Lectionary
Advent 2026 to the eve of Advent 2027 (Year B)

Church House Publishing

Published by	Church House Publishing Church House Great Smith Street London SW1P 3AZ
Compilation ©	*The Archbishops' Council 2026*
ISBN	978-0-7151-2456-7 Standard 978-0-7151-2466-6 Large 978-0-7151-2476-5 E-ISBN
All rights reserved	No part of this publication may be reproduced in any form or by any means, electronic or mechanical, including photocopying, recording, or any information storage and retrieval system, except as stated below, without written permission which should be sought from the Copyright Administrator, The Archbishops' Council, Church House, Great Smith Street, London SW1P 3AZ Email: copyright@churchofengland.org
Authorization	The Common Worship Calendar and Lectionaries are authorized pursuant to Canon B 2 of the Canons of the Church of England for use until further resolution of the General Synod of the Church of England.
Copyright and Acknowledgements	The Revised Common Lectionary is copyright © The Consultation on Common Texts: 1992. The Church of England adaptations to the Principal Service Lectionary are copyright © The Archbishops' Council, as are the Second and Third Service Lectionaries, the Weekday Lectionary for Morning and Evening Prayer and the Additional Weekday Lectionary. The Daily Eucharistic Lectionary derives, with some adaptation, from the Ordo Lectionum Missae of the Roman Catholic Church and is reproduced by permission of The International Commission on English in the Liturgy. EU GPSR Authorised Representative LOGOS EUROPE, 9 rue Nicolas Poussin, 17000, LA ROCHELLE, France E-mail: Contact@logoseurope.eu No part of this book may be used or reproduced in any manner for the purpose of training artificial intelligence technologies or systems. Edited by Peter Moger Designed by Derek Birdsall & John Morgan/Omnific Typeset by RefineCatch Ltd, Bungay, Suffolk Printed in England by Core Publications Ltd

Contents of this booklet

This booklet gives details of the full range of possibilities envisaged in the liturgical calendar and lectionary of Common Worship. Its use as a tool for the preparation of worship will require the making of several choices based first on the general celebration of the Christian year by the Church of England as a whole; second on the customary pattern of calendar in the diocese, parish and place of worship; and third on the pattern of services locally.

The **first column** comprises the Calendar of the Church with the days of the year. Observances that are mandatory are printed either in **bold** type (Sundays), in **bold** type (Principal Feasts and Holy Days) or in roman (Festivals). Optional celebrations (Lesser Festivals) and Commemorations are printed in ordinary roman type and *italic* type respectively.

The **second column** comprises (a) the readings and psalms for the Principal Service on Sundays, Principal Feasts and Holy Days, and Festivals, and (b) Holy Communion readings and psalms for other days of the week. On the Sundays after Trinity, the Old Testament reading and its psalm are divided into two smaller columns, indicating a choice between a 'continuous' reading week by week or a reading 'related' to the Gospel for that day.

The **third column** comprises (a) the Third Service readings and psalms for Sundays, Principal Feasts and Holy Days, and Festivals, and (b) the readings and psalms for weekday Morning Prayer.

The **fourth column** comprises (a) the Second Service readings and psalms for Sundays, Principal Feasts and Holy Days, and Festivals, and (b) the readings and psalms for weekday Evening Prayer.

An **Additional Weekday Lectionary**, intended particularly for use in places of worship that attract occasional rather than daily worshippers, is provided on pages 72–79. It may be used either at Morning or Evening Prayer.

Common of the Saints

General readings and psalms for saints' days can be found on pages 81–85; for some particular celebrations, other readings are suggested there.

Special Occasions

Readings and psalms for special occasions can be found on pages 86–87.

Liturgical colours

Appropriate liturgical colours are suggested in this booklet. They are not mandatory; traditional or local use may be followed.

Colours are indicated by single letters: the first (always upper case) for the season or Festival; and occasionally a second (lower case) for an optional celebration on that day. Thus, for example, *Gr* for the celebration of a Lesser Festival whose liturgical colour is red, in an otherwise 'green' season.

The following abbreviations are used:

G	Green
P or p	Purple or Violet
P(La)	Purple or Lent array
R or r	Red
W or w	White (Gold is indicated where its use would be appropriate)

Notes on the Lectionary

Sundays, Principal Feasts and Holy Days and Festivals

Three sets of psalms and readings are provided for each Sunday, Principal Feast or Holy Day and Festival.

The **Principal Service lectionary** (based on the Revised Common Lectionary) is intended for use at the principal service of the day (whether this service is Holy Communion or some other authorized form). In most Church communities, this is likely to be the mid-morning service, but the minister is free to decide which service time normally constitutes the Principal Service of the day. This lectionary may be used twice if required – for example, at an early celebration of Holy Communion and then again at a later one.

If only **two readings** are used at the Principal Service and that service is Holy Communion, the second reading must always be the Gospel reading. When the Principal Service lectionary is used at a service other than Holy Communion, the Gospel reading need not always be chosen.

The **Second Service lectionary** is intended for a second main service. In many churches, this lectionary may be the appropriate provision for a Sunday afternoon or evening service. A Gospel reading is always provided so that this lectionary can, if necessary, be used where the second main service is a celebration of Holy Communion.

The **Third Service lectionary**, with shorter readings, is intended where a third set of psalms and readings is needed and is most appropriate for use at an office. A Gospel reading is not always provided, so this lectionary is not suitable for use at Holy Communion.

Weekdays

The Common Worship Weekday Lectionary authorized by the General Synod in 2005 comprises a lectionary (with psalms) for Holy Communion, a lectionary for Morning and Evening Prayer, and tables of psalms for Morning and Evening Prayer.

The **Daily Eucharistic Lectionary** (based on the Roman Catholic daily eucharistic lectionary) is a semi-continuous two-year lectionary with a wide use of scripture, though not complete coverage of the Bible. Two readings are provided for each day, the first from either the Old or New Testament, the second always a Gospel. Psalm provision is intended to be a brief response to the first reading. It is for use at Holy Communion normally in places with a daily or near-daily celebration with a regular congregation. It may also be used as an office lectionary.

The **lectionary for Morning and Evening Prayer** always provides two readings for each office, the first from the Old Testament and the second from the New Testament. These are generally in sequence. One of the New Testament readings for any particular day is from the Gospels.

The psalms for Morning and Evening Prayer follow a sequential pattern in Ordinary Time (apart from the period from All Saints to the beginning of Advent).

In the periods from All Saints until 18 December, from the Epiphany until the Presentation of Christ in the Temple (Candlemas), from Ash Wednesday until Palm Sunday, and from the Monday after Easter Week until Pentecost, there is a choice of psalms at Morning and Evening Prayer. The psalms printed first reflect the theme of the season. Alternatively, the psalms from the Ordinary Time cycle may be used. The two sets are separated by '*or*'.

From 19 December until the Epiphany and from the Monday of Holy Week until the Saturday of Easter Week, only seasonal psalms are provided.

Where more than one psalm is given, one psalm (printed in **bold**) may be used as the sole psalm at that office.

Guidance on how these options for saying the psalms are expressed typographically can be found in the 'Notes on the Lectionary' below.

A further cycle is provided (see table on page 88), which is largely the monthly sequential cycle of psalms given in the *Book of Common Prayer*.

A single psalm for use by those who only say one office each day is provided in Prayer During the Day in *Common Worship: Daily Prayer*.

An **Additional Weekday Lectionary**, intended particularly for use in places of worship that attract occasional rather than daily worshippers, is provided on pages 72–79. It can be used either at Morning or Evening Prayer. Psalmody is not provided and should be taken from provision outlined above.

Using the Lectionary tables

All **Bible references** (except to the Psalms) are to the *New Revised Standard Version* (New York, 1989). Those who use other Bible translations should check the verse numbers against the *NRSV*. Each reference gives book, chapter and verse, in that order.

References to the Psalms are to the Common Worship psalter, published in *Common Worship: Services and Prayers for the Church of England* (2000) and *Common Worship: Daily Prayer* (2005). A table showing the verse number differences between this and the psalter in the *Book of Common Prayer* is provided on the Common Worship website https://www.churchofengland.org/prayer-and-worship/worship-texts-and-resources/common-worship/daily-prayer/psalter/psalter-verse).

Options in the provision of readings or psalms are presented in the following ways:
- ¶ square brackets [xx] give either optional additional verses or Psalms, or a shorter alternative;
- ¶ '*or*' indicates a simple choice between two alternative readings or courses of psalms;
- ¶ a psalm printed in **bold** may be used as the sole psalm at that office;
- ¶ on weekdays a psalm printed in parentheses (xx) is omitted if it has been used as the opening canticle at that office;
- ¶ a psalm marked with an asterisk may be shortened if desired.

Where a reading from the **Apocrypha** is offered, an alternative Old Testament reading is provided.

In the choice of **readings other than the Gospel** reading, the minister should ensure that, in any year, a balance is maintained between readings from the Old and New Testaments and that, where a particular biblical book is appointed to be read over several weeks, the choice ensures that the continuity of one book is not lost.

On the Sundays after Trinity, the Principal Service Lectionary provides **alternative Old Testament readings and psalms**. References in the left-hand column (under the heading 'Continuous') offer a *semi-continuous* reading of Old Testament texts. Such a reading and its complementary psalmody stand independently of the other readings. References in the right-hand column (under the heading 'Related') *relate* the Old Testament reading and the psalm to the Gospel reading. One column should be followed for the whole sequence of Sundays after Trinity.

The Lectionary 2026–2027

The Sunday and festal readings for 29 November 2026 (the First Sunday of Advent) to 27 November 2027 (the eve of Advent Sunday) are from **Year B**, which offers a semi-continuous reading of Mark's Gospel at the Principal Service on Sundays throughout the year.

The weekday readings for Holy Communion are from **Year One** of the Daily Eucharistic Lectionary (DEL).

Office readings are from Table 2 of the Weekday Lectionary: Old Testament 2a in both Seasonal Time and Ordinary Time, and New Testament 2 at Morning Prayer, and from Table 1 of the Weekday Lectionary at Evening Prayer.

Notes on the Calendar 29 November 2026— 27 November 2027

These notes are based on the Rules to Order the Christian Year (*Common Worship: Times and Seasons*, pages 24–30).

Sundays

All Sundays celebrate the paschal mystery of the death and resurrection of the Lord. They also reflect the character of the seasons in which they are set.

Principal Feasts

On these days (printed in **bold**) Holy Communion is celebrated in every cathedral and in at least one church in each benefice or, where benefices are held in plurality, in at least one church in at least one of those benefices, and this celebration, required by Canon B 14, may not be displaced by any other celebration, and may be dispensed with only in accordance with the provision of Canon B 14A.

Except in the case of Christmas Day and Easter Day, the celebration of the Feast *begins with Evening Prayer on the day before the Feast*, and the Collect at that Evening Prayer is that of the Feast. In the case of Christmas Eve and Easter Eve, there is proper liturgical provision (including a Collect) for the whole day.

The Epiphany may, for pastoral reasons, be celebrated on Sunday 3 January. **The Presentation of Christ in the Temple** (Candlemas) is celebrated on either Monday 2 February or Sunday 31 January.

Other Principal Holy Days

These days (printed in **bold**), and the liturgical provision for them, may not be displaced by any other celebration.

Ash Wednesday (10 February) and **Maundy Thursday** (25 March) are Principal Holy Days. On both these days Holy Communion is celebrated in every cathedral or in at least one church in each benefice or, where benefices are held in plurality, in at least one church in at least one of those benefices, except where there is dispensation under Canon B 14A.

Good Friday (26 March) is a Principal Holy Day.

Eastertide

The paschal character of **the Great Fifty Days of Easter**, from Easter Day (28 March) to Pentecost (16 May), should be celebrated throughout the season, and should not be displaced by other celebrations. No Festival day may be celebrated in Easter Week; and nor may any Festival – except for a Patronal or Dedication Festival – displace the celebration of a Sunday (a memorial of the resurrection) during Eastertide. The paschal character of the season should be retained on those weekdays when saints' days are celebrated.

The three days before Ascension Day (3–5 May) are customarily observed as **Rogation Days**, when prayer is offered for God's blessing on the fruits of the earth and on human labour.

The nine days **after Ascension Day until the eve of Pentecost** (7–15 May) are observed as days of prayer and preparation for the celebration of the outpouring of the Holy Spirit.

Ordinary Time

Ordinary Time comprises two periods in the year: first, the period from the day after the Presentation of Christ in the Temple until the day before Ash Wednesday, and second, that from the day after Pentecost until the day before the First Sunday of Advent.

During Ordinary Time, there is no seasonal emphasis, except that the period between All Saints' Day and the First Sunday of Advent is a time to celebrate and reflect upon the reign of Christ in earth and heaven.

Festivals

These days (printed in roman), and the liturgical provision for them, are not usually displaced. For each day there is full liturgical provision for a Principal, Second and Third Service, and an optional so-called First Evening Prayer on the evening before the Festival where this is required.

Festivals may *not* be celebrated on Sundays in Advent, Lent or Eastertide, the Baptism of Christ, Ascension Day, Trinity Sunday or Christ the King, or weekdays between Palm Sunday and the Second Sunday of Easter.

Otherwise, a Festival falling on a Sunday – namely in 2026–27, James the Apostle (falling on the Ninth Sunday after Trinity) and The Blessed Virgin Mary (falling on the Twelfth Sunday after Trinity) – may be kept on that Sunday or transferred to the Monday (or, at the discretion of the minister, to the next suitable weekday). John the Evangelist (falling on the First Sunday of Christmas) may be transferred to Tuesday 29 December 2026.

Certain Festivals (namely, Matthias the Apostle, the Visit of the Blessed Virgin Mary to Elizabeth, Thomas the Apostle, and The Blessed Virgin Mary) have customary alternative dates (see p.8).

The Thursday after Trinity Sunday (27 May) may be observed as the **Day of Thanksgiving for the Institution of Holy Communion** (sometimes known as *Corpus Christi*), and may be kept as a Festival.

Other Celebrations

Mothering Sunday falls on the Fourth Sunday of Lent (7 March). Alternative prayers and readings are provided for the Principal Service. **Bible Sunday** may be celebrated on 24 October, replacing the Last Sunday after Trinity, and appropriate prayers and readings are provided.

Local Celebrations

The celebration of **the patron saint or the title of a church** is kept either as a Festival or as a Principal Feast.

The **Dedication Festival** of a church is the anniversary of the date of its dedication or consecration. This is kept either as a Festival or as a Principal Feast. When kept as Principal Feasts, the Patronal and Dedication Festivals may be transferred to the nearest Sunday, unless that day is already a Principal Feast or one of the following days: the First Sunday of Advent, the Baptism of Christ, the First Sunday of Lent, the Fifth Sunday of Lent, or Palm Sunday. If the actual date is not known, the Dedication Festival may be celebrated on 3 October (replacing the Nineteenth Sunday after Trinity), or on 24 October (replacing the Last Sunday after Trinity), or on a suitable date chosen locally. Readings can be found on page 80.

Harvest Thanksgiving may be celebrated on any Sunday in autumn, replacing the provision for that day, provided it does not displace any Principal Feast or Festival.

Diocesan and other local provision may be made in **the calendar of the saints** to supplement the general calendar, in accordance with Canon B 6, paragraph 5.

Lesser Festivals

Lesser Festivals (printed in ordinary roman type, in black) are observed in a manner appropriate to a particular place. Each is provided with a Collect, which may supersede the Collect of the week. For certain Lesser Festivals a complete set of Eucharistic readings is provided, and for others appropriate readings may be selected from the Common of the Saints (see pages 81–85). These readings may, at the minister's discretion, supersede the Daily Eucharistic Lectionary (DEL). The weekday psalms and readings at Morning and Evening Prayer are not usually superseded by those for Lesser Festivals, but at the minister's discretion psalms and readings provided on these days for use at Holy Communion may be used instead at Morning or Evening Prayer.

The minister may be selective in the Lesser Festivals that are observed and may also keep some, or all of them, as Commemorations, perhaps especially in Advent, Lent and Easter where the character of the season ought to be sustained. If the Day of Thanksgiving for the Institution of Holy Communion (27 May) is not kept as a Festival in 2026, it may be kept as a Lesser Festival.

When a Lesser Festival falls on a Principal Feast or Holy Day, a Festival, a Sunday, or on a weekday between Palm Sunday and the Second Sunday of Easter, its celebration is normally omitted for that year. However, where there is sufficient reason, it may, at the discretion of the minister, be celebrated on the nearest available day.

Commemorations

Commemorations (printed in *italic*) are made by a mention in prayers of intercession. They are not provided with Collect, Psalm and Readings, and do not replace the usual weekday provision at Holy Communion or at Morning and Evening Prayer.

The minister may be selective in the Commemorations that are made.

Only where there is an established celebration in the wider Church or where the day has a special local significance may a Commemoration be observed as a Lesser Festival, with liturgical provision from the Common of the Saints (pages 81–85).

In designating a Commemoration as a Lesser Festival, the minister must remember the need to maintain the spirit of the season, especially of Advent, Lent and Easter.

Days of Discipline and Self-Denial

The weekdays of Lent and every Friday in the year are days of discipline and self-denial, with the exception of Principal Feasts, Festivals outside Lent, and Fridays from Easter Day to Pentecost. The day preceding a Principal Feast may also be appropriately kept as a day of discipline and self-denial in preparation for the Feast.

Ember Days

Ember Days should be kept, under the bishop's directions, in the week before an ordination as days of prayer for those to be ordained deacon or priest.

Ember Days may also be kept even when there is no ordination in the diocese as more general days of prayer for those who serve the Church in its various ministries, both ordained and lay, and for vocations. Traditionally they have been observed on the Wednesday, Friday and Saturday in the week before the Third Sunday of Advent, the Second Sunday of Lent, and the Sundays nearest to 29 June and 29 September.

Notes on Collects

For a table showing where the Collects and Post Communions are published, see page 80.

Where a Collect ends 'through Jesus Christ … now and for ever', the minister may omit the longer (trinitarian) ending and use the shorter ending, 'through Jesus Christ our Lord', to which the people respond, 'Amen'. The longer ending, however, is to be preferred at a service of Holy Communion.

The Collect for each Sunday is used at Evening Prayer on the Saturday preceding, except where that Saturday is a Principal Feast, or a Festival, or the eve of Christmas Day or Easter Day. The Collect for each Sunday is also used on the weekdays following, except where other provision is made.

Abbreviations used in this book

Alt	Alternative		P or p	Purple or Violet
BVM	Blessed Virgin Mary		P(La)	Purple or Lent Array
DEL	Daily Eucharistic Lectionary		Ps & Pss	Psalmody
EP	Evening Prayer		R or r	Red
G	Green		W or w	White (Gold is indicated where its use would be appropriate)

HC Holy Communion: used where additional references are given to provide alternative texts for use at a celebration of Holy Communion (most often the provision of a psalm or gospel)

MP Morning Prayer

Alternative dates

The following may be celebrated on the alternative dates indicated:

Thomas the Apostle –
on 21 December 2026 instead of 3 July 2027

Matthias the Apostle –
on 24 February instead of 14 May

The Visit of the Blessed Virgin Mary to Elizabeth –
on 2 July instead of 31 May

Thomas Becket –
on 7 July 2026 instead of 29 December 2025

Cuthbert –
on 4 September instead of 20 March

The Blessed Virgin Mary –
on 8 September instead of 15 August

Chad – with Cedd
on 26 October instead of 2 March

If any of the four festivals is celebrated on the alternative date these provisions should be used on the principal date:

Holy Communion	Morning Prayer	Evening Prayer

If Thomas the Apostle is celebrated on Monday 21 December 2026 the following provision is used on Saturday 3 July 2027 (G):

Genesis 27.1–5a, 15–29	Psalms 120, **121**, 122	Psalm **118**
Psalm 135.1–6	Esther 3	1 Samuel 4.1b–end
Matthew 9.14–17	2 Corinthians 5	Luke 20.27–40

If Matthias the Apostle is celebrated on Wednesday 24 February the following provision is used on Friday 14 May (W):

Acts 25.13–21	Psalms **28**, 30 or **139**	Psalms **147** or **130**, 131, 137
Psalm 103.1–2, 11–12, 19–20	Deuteronomy 33	Numbers 27.12–end
John 21.15–19	1 John 4.7–end	Luke 8.40–end
	*Ezekiel 36.22–28; Matthew 12.22–32	

If The Visit of the Blessed Virgin Mary to Elizabeth is celebrated on Friday 2 July the following provision is used on Monday 31 May (G):

Tobit 1.1, 2, 2.1–8 or 1 Peter 1.3–9	Psalms 27, **30**	Psalms 26, **28**, 29
Psalm 15 or 111	2 Chronicles 33.1–13	Joshua 14
Mark 12.1–12	Romans 7.1–6	Luke 12.1–12

If The Blessed Virgin Mary is celebrated on Wednesday 8 September the following provision is used on Sunday 15 August (G):

Principal Service	3rd Service	2nd Service

12th Sunday after Trinity
Proper 15
Continuous:
1 Kings 2.10–12; 3.3–14
Psalm 111

Related:
Proverbs 9.1–6
Psalm 34.9–14

Ephesians 5.15–20
John 6.51–58

Psalm 106.1–10
Jonah 1
or Ecclesiasticus 3.1–15
2 Peter 3.14–end
HC Luke 12.49–56

Psalms [92] 100
Exodus 2.23—3.10
Hebrews 13.1–15

Key to the Tables

For guidance on how the options for saying the psalms are expressed typographically, see page 5.

Sundays (and Principal Feasts, other Principal Holy Days, and Festivals)

Day	Date	Colour	Principal Service	3rd Service	2nd Service
	Sunday / **Feast** † / Festival ‡‡		Main service of the day: Holy Communion, Morning Prayer, Evening Prayer, or a Service of the Word	Shorter Readings, an Office lectionary probably used at Morning Prayer where Holy Communion is the Principal Service	2nd main service, probably used at Evening Prayer; adaptable for Holy Communion

† Principal Feasts and other Principal Holy Days are printed in **bold**.
‡‡ Festivals are printed in roman typeface.

Weekdays

Day	Date	Colour	Holy Communion	Morning Prayer	Evening Prayer
			Weekday readings	Psalms and readings for Morning Prayer	Psalms and readings for Evening Prayer

Lesser Festival ‡* [optional]
Commemoration ‡‡ [optional]

‡ Lesser Festivals are printed in roman typeface, in black.
‡‡ Commemorations are printed in *italics*.
* The ascriptions given to holy men and women in the Calendar (such as martyr, teacher of the faith, etc.) have often been abbreviated in this booklet for reasons of space. The particular ascription given is there to be helpful if needing to choose Collects and readings from Common of the Saints; where several ascriptions are used (e.g. bishop and martyr), traditionally the last ascription given is the most important and therefore the guiding one. The full ascriptions may be found in the Calendar, which is printed in *Common Worship: Times and Seasons* (pages 7–22), *Common Worship: Festivals* (pages 5–20) and *Common Worship: Daily Prayer* (pages 5–16).
These incorporate minor corrections made since the publication of the Calendar in *Common Worship: Services and Prayers for the Church of England* (pages 5–16).

Advent 1

		Principal Service	3rd Service	2nd Service
Sunday	**29 November** *P* **1st Sunday of Advent**	Isaiah 64.1–9 Psalm 80.1–8, 18–20 [or 80.1–8] 1 Corinthians 1.3–9 Mark 13.24–end	Psalm 44 Isaiah 2.1–5 Luke 12.35–48	Psalm 25 [or 25.1–9] Isaiah 1.1–20 Matthew 21.1–13 or: 1st EP of Andrew the Apostle: Psalm 48; Isaiah 49.1–9a; 1 Corinthians 4.9–16
Monday	**30 November** *R* Andrew the Apostle	Isaiah 52.7–10 Psalm 19.1–6 Romans 10.12–18 Matthew 4.18–22	MP Psalms 47, 147.1–12 Ezekiel 47.1–12 or Ecclesiasticus 14.20–end John 12.20–32	EP Psalms 87, 96 Zechariah 8.20–end John 1.35–42
		Holy Communion	**Morning Prayer**	**Evening Prayer**
Tuesday	**1 December** *P* *Charles de Foucauld, hermit, 1916*	Isaiah 11.1–10 Psalm 72.1–4, 18–19 Luke 10.2–24	Psalms **80**, 82 or **5**, 6 (8) Isaiah 43.1–13 Revelation 20	Psalms **74**, 75 or **9**, 10* Isaiah 26.1–13 Matthew 12.22–37
Wednesday	**2 December** *P*	Isaiah 25.6–10a Psalm 23 Matthew 15.29–37	Psalms 5, **7** or 119.1–32 Isaiah 43.14–end Revelation 21.1–8	Psalms 76, **77** or **11**, 12, 13 Isaiah 28.1–13 Matthew 12.38–end
Thursday	**3 December** *P* *Francis Xavier, missionary, 1552*	Isaiah 26.1–6 Psalm 118.18–27a Matthew 7.21, 24–27	Psalms 42, 43 or 14, **15**, 16 Isaiah 44.1–8 Revelation 21.9–21	Psalms **40**, 46 or **18*** Isaiah 28.14–end Matthew 13.1–23
Friday	**4 December** *P* *John of Damascus, monk,* *teacher of the faith, c.749* *Nicholas Ferrar, deacon, founder of the* *Little Gidding Community, 1637*	Isaiah 29.17–end Psalm 27.1–4, 16–17 Matthew 9.27–31	Psalms **25**, 26 or 17, **19** Isaiah 44.9–23 Revelation 21.22—22.5	Psalms 16, 17 or **22** Isaiah 29.1–14 Matthew 13.24–43
Saturday	**5 December** *P*	Isaiah 30.19–21, 23–26 Psalm 146.4–9 Matthew 9.35—10.1, 6–8	Psalms **9** (10) or 20, 21, **23** Isaiah 44.24—45.13 Revelation 22.6–end	Psalms **27**, 28 or **24**, 25 Isaiah 29.15–end Matthew 13.44–end

Advent 2

		Principal Service	3rd Service	2nd Service
Sunday	**6 December** P **2nd Sunday of Advent**	Isaiah 40.1–11 Psalm 85.1–2, 8–end [or 85.8–end] 2 Peter 3.8–15a Mark 1.1–8	Psalm 80 Baruch 5.1–9 or Zephaniah 3.14–end Luke 1.5–20	Psalm 40 [or 40.12–end] 1 Kings 22.1–28 Romans 15.4–13 HC Matthew 11.2–11
		Holy Communion	**Morning Prayer**	**Evening Prayer**
Monday	**7 December** Pw Ambrose, bishop, teacher of the faith, 397 (see p.82)	Isaiah 35 Psalm 85.7–end Luke 5.17–26	Psalm 44 or 27, 30 Isaiah 45.14–end 1 Thessalonians 1	Psalms 144, 146 or 26, **28**, 29 Isaiah 30.1–18 Matthew 14.1–12
Tuesday	**8 December** Pw Conception of the Blessed Virgin Mary (see p.81)	Isaiah 40.1–11 Psalm 96.1, 10–end Matthew 18.12–14	Psalms 56, 57 or 32, **36** Isaiah 46 1 Thessalonians 2.1–12	Psalms 11, 12, 13 or **33** Isaiah 30.19–end Matthew 14.13–end
Wednesday	**9 December** P Ember Day	Isaiah 40.25–end Psalm 103.8–13 Matthew 11.28–end	Psalms **62**, 63 or **34** Isaiah 47 1 Thessalonians 2.13–end	Psalms 10, 14 or 119.33–56 Isaiah 31 Matthew 15.1–20
Thursday	**10 December** P	Isaiah 41.13–20 Psalm 145.1, 8–13 Matthew 11.11–15	Psalms 53, **54**, 60 or **37*** Isaiah 48.1–11 1 Thessalonians 3	Psalm 73 or 39, **40** Isaiah 32 Matthew 15.21–28
Friday	**11 December** P Ember Day	Isaiah 48.17–19 Psalm 1 Matthew 11.16–19	Psalms 85, **86** or 31 Isaiah 48.12–end 1 Thessalonians 4.1–12	Psalms 82, **90** or 35 Isaiah 33.1–22 Matthew 15.29–end
Saturday	**12 December** P Ember Day	Ecclesiasticus 48.1–4, 9–11 or 2 Kings 2.9–12 Psalm 80.1–4, 18–19 Matthew 17.10–13	Psalm 145 or 41, **42**, 43 Isaiah 49.1–13 1 Thessalonians 4.13–end	Psalms 93, **94** or 45, **46** Isaiah 35 Matthew 16.1–12

Advent 3

		Principal Service	3rd Service	2nd Service
Sunday	**13 December** P 3rd Sunday of Advent	Isaiah 61.1–4, 8–end Psalm 126 or *Canticle*: Magnificat 1 Thessalonians 5.16–24 John 1.6–8, 19–28	Psalms 50.1–6, 62 Isaiah 12 Luke 1.57–66	Psalm 68.1–19 [or 68.1–8] Malachi 3.1—4.4 Philippians 4.4–7 HC Matthew 14.1–12
		Holy Communion	**Morning Prayer**	**Evening Prayer**
Monday	**14 December** Pw John of the Cross, poet, teacher of the faith, 1591 (see p.82)	Numbers 24.2–7, 15–17 Psalm 25.3–8 Matthew 21.23–27	Psalm **40** or **44** Isaiah 49.14–25 1 Thessalonians 5.1–11	Psalms 25, **26** or **47**, 49 Isaiah 38.1–8, 21–22 Matthew 16.13–end
Tuesday	**15 December** P	Zephaniah 3.1–2, 9–13 Psalm 34.1–6, 21–22 Matthew 21.28–32	Psalms **70**, 74 or **48**, 52 Isaiah 50 1 Thessalonians 5.12–end	Psalms **50**, 54 or **50** Isaiah 38. 9–20 Matthew 17.1–13
Wednesday	**16 December** P	Isaiah 45.6b–8, 18, 21b–end Psalm 85.7–end Luke 7.18b–23	Psalms **75**, 96 or 119. **57–80** Isaiah 51.1–8 2 Thessalonians 1	Psalms 25, **82** or **59**, 60, (67) Isaiah 39 Matthew 17.14–21
Thursday	**17 December** P *O Sapientia* Eglantyne Jebb, social reformer, founder of 'Save The Children', 1928	Genesis 49.2, 8–10 Psalm 72.1–5, 18–19 Matthew 1.1–17	Psalms **76**, 97 or 56, **57**, (63*) Isaiah 51.9–16 2 Thessalonians 2	Psalms **44** or 61, **62**, 64 Zephaniah 1.1—2.3 Matthew 17.22–end
Friday	**18 December** P *O Adonai*	Jeremiah 23.5–8 Psalm 72.1–2, 12–13, 18–end Matthew 1.18–24	Psalms 77, **98** or **51**, **54** Isaiah 51.17–end 2 Thessalonians 3	Psalm **49** or **38** Zephaniah 3.1–13 Matthew 18.1–20
			From Saturday 19 December until the Epiphany *the seasonal psalmody must be used at Morning and Evening Prayer.*	
Saturday	**19 December** P *O Radix Jesse*	Judges 13.2–7, 24–end Psalm 71.3–8 Luke 1.5–25	Psalms 144, **146** Isaiah 52.1–12 Jude	Psalms 10, **57** Zephaniah 3.14–end Matthew 18.21–end

Advent 4

		Principal Service	3rd Service	2nd Service
Sunday	**20 December** P **4th Sunday of Advent** *O Clavis David*	2 Samuel 7.1–11,16 Canticle: Magnificat or Psalm 89.1–4, 19–26 [or 89.1–8] Romans 16.25–end Luke 1.26–38	Psalm 144 Isaiah 7.10–16 Romans 1.1–7	Psalms 113 [131] Zechariah 2.10–end Luke 1.39–55
		Holy Communion	**Morning Prayer**	**Evening Prayer**
Monday	**21 December** P *O Oriens*	Zephaniah 3.14–18 Psalm 33.1–4, 11–12, 20–end Luke 1.39–45	Psalms 121, 122, 123 Isaiah 52.13—end of 53 2 Peter 1.1–15	Psalms 80, **84** Malachi 1.1, 6–end Matthew 19.1–12
Tuesday	**22 December** P *O Rex Gentium*	1 Samuel 1.24–end Psalm 113 Luke 1.46–56	Psalms **124**, 125, 126, 127 Isaiah 54 2 Peter 1.16—2.3	Psalms 24, **48** Malachi 2.1–16 Matthew 19.13–15
Wednesday	**23 December** P *O Emmanuel*	Malachi 3.1–4, 4.5–end Psalm 25.3–9 Luke 1.57–66	Psalms 128, 129, **130**, 131 Isaiah 55 2 Peter 2.4–end	Psalm 89.1–37 Malachi 2.17—3.12 Matthew 19.16–end
Thursday	**24 December** P **Christmas Eve**	2 Samuel 7.1–5, 8–11, 16 Psalm 89.2, 19–27 Acts 13.16–26 Luke 1.67–79	Psalms **45**, 113 Isaiah 56.1–8 2 Peter 3	Psalm 85 Zechariah 2 Revelation 1.1–8
		Principal Service	**3rd Service**	**2nd Service**
Friday	**25 December** **Christmas Day**	*Gold or W* Any of the following three sets of Principal Service readings may be used on the evening of Christmas Eve and on Christmas Day. Set III should be used at some service during the celebration. **Set I** Isaiah 9.2–7 Psalm 96 Titus 2.11–14 Luke 2.1–14 [15–20] **Set II** Isaiah 62.6–end Psalm 97 Titus 3.4–7 Luke 2. [1–7] 8–20 **Set III** Isaiah 52.7–10 Psalm 98 Hebrews 1.1–4 [5–12] John 1.1–14	MP Psalms **110**, 117 Isaiah 62.1–5 Matthew 1.18–end	EP Psalm **8** Isaiah 65.17–25 Philippians 2.5–11 or Luke 2.1–20 if it has not been used at the principal service of the day
Saturday	**26 December** R Stephen, deacon, first martyr	2 Chronicles 24.20–22 or Acts 7.51–end Psalm 119.161–168 Acts 7.51–end or Galatians 2.16b–20 Matthew 10.17–22	MP Psalms **13**, 31.1–8, 150 Jeremiah 26.12–15 Acts 6	EP Psalms 57, **86** Genesis 4.1–10 Matthew 23.34–end

John, Apostle and Evangelist / Christmas 1

If John, Apostle and Evangelist is celebrated on Sunday 27 December:

		Principal Service	3rd Service	2nd Service
Sunday	**27 December** W John, Apostle and Evangelist	Exodus 33.7–11a Psalm 117 1 John 1 John 21.19b–end	MP Psalms **21**, 147.13–end Exodus 33.12–end 1 John 2.1–11	EP Psalm **97** Isaiah 6.1–8 1 John 5.1–12
Monday	**28 December** R The Holy Innocents	Jeremiah 31.15–17 Psalm 124 1 Corinthians 1.26–29 Matthew 2.13–18	MP Psalms **36**, 146 Baruch 4.21–27 or Genesis 37.13–20 Matthew 18.1–10	EP Psalms 123, **128** Isaiah 49.14–25 Mark 10.13–16
		Holy Communion	**Morning Prayer**	**Evening Prayer**
Tuesday	**29 December** Wr Thomas Becket, archbishop, martyr, 1170 (see p.81)	1 John 2.3–11 Psalm 96.1–4 Luke 2.22–35	Psalms **19**, 20 Isaiah 57.15–end John 1.1–18	Psalms 131, **132** Jonah 1 Colossians 1.1–14

If John, Apostle and Evangelist is transferred to Tuesday 29 December:

		Principal Service	3rd Service	2nd Service
Sunday	**27 December** W 1st Sunday of Christmas	Isaiah 61.10—62.3 Psalm 148 [or 148.7–end] Galatians 4.4–7 Luke 2.15–21	Psalm 105.1–11 Isaiah 63.7–9 Ephesians 3.5–12	Psalm 132 Isaiah 35 Colossians 1.9–20 or Luke 2.41–end
Monday	**28 December** R The Holy Innocents	Jeremiah 31.15–17 Psalm 124 1 Corinthians 1.26–29 Matthew 2.13–18	MP Psalms **36**, 146 Baruch 4.21–27 or Genesis 37.13–20 Matthew 18.1–10	EP Psalms 123, **128** Isaiah 49.14–25 Mark 10.13–16
Tuesday	**29 December** W John, Apostle and Evangelist	Exodus 33.7–11a Psalm 117 1 John 1 John 21.19b–end	MP Psalms **21**, 147.13–end Exodus 33.12–end 1 John 2.1–11	EP Psalm **97** Isaiah 6.1–8 1 John 5.1–12

Christmas 1

			Holy Communion	Morning Prayer	Evening Prayer
Wednesday	**30 December**	W	1 John 2.12–17 Psalm 96.7–10 Luke 2.36–40	Psalms 111, 112, 113 Isaiah 59.1–15a John 1.19–28	Psalms **65**, 84 Jonah 2 Colossians 1.15–23
Thursday	**31 December** *John Wyclif, reformer, 1384*	W	1 John 2.18–21 Psalm 96.1, 11–end John 1.1–18	Psalm **102** Isaiah 59.15b–end John 1.29–34	Psalms **90**, 148 Jonah 3–4 Colossians 1.24—2.7 *or:* 1st EP of the Naming and Circumcision of Jesus: Psalm 148; Jeremiah 23.1–6; Colossians 2.8–15

			Principal Service	3rd Service	2nd Service
Friday	**1 January** Naming and Circumcision of Jesus	W	Numbers 6.22–end Psalm 8 Galatians 4.4–7 Luke 2.15–21	*MP* Psalms **103**, 150 Genesis 17.1–13 Romans 2.17–end	*EP* Psalm 115 Deuteronomy 30.[1–10] 11–end Acts 3.1–16

Christmas 2 / Epiphany

If the Epiphany is celebrated on Wednesday 6 January:

			Holy Communion	Morning Prayer	Evening Prayer
Saturday	**2 January** Basil the Great and Gregory of Nazianzus, bishops, teachers of the faith, 379 and 389 (see p.82) *Seraphim, monk, spiritual guide, 1833* *Vedanayagam Samuel Azariah, bishop, evangelist, 1945*	W	1 John 2.22–28 Psalm 98.1–4 John 1.19–28	Psalm **18.1–30** Isaiah 60.1–12 John 1.35–42	Psalms 45, **46** Ruth 1 Colossians 2.8–end
			Principal Service	**3rd Service**	**2nd Service**
Sunday	**3 January** **2nd Sunday of Christmas**	W	Jeremiah 31.7–14 *or* Ecclesiasticus 24.1–12 Psalm 147.13–end *or Canticle:* Wisdom 10.15–end Ephesians 1.3–14 John 1.[1–9] 10–18	Psalm 87 Zechariah 8.1–8 Luke 2.41–end	Psalm 135 [*or* 135.1–14] Isaiah 46.3–end Romans 12.1–8 HC Matthew 2.13–end
			Holy Communion	**Morning Prayer**	**Evening Prayer**
Monday	**4 January**	W	1 John 3.7–10 Psalm 98.1, 8–end John 1.35–42	Psalm **89.1–37** Isaiah 61 John 2.1–12	Psalms 85, **87** Ruth 3 Colossians 3.12—4.1
Tuesday	**5 January**	W	1 John 3.11–21 Psalm 100 John 1.43–end	Psalms 8, **48** Isaiah 62 John 2.13–end	**1st EP of the Epiphany** Psalms 96, **97**; Isaiah 49.1–13 John 4.7–26
			Principal Service	**3rd Service**	**2nd Service**
Wednesday	**6 January** **Epiphany**	*Gold or W*	Isaiah 60.1–6 Psalm 72. [1–9] 10–15 Ephesians 3.1–12 Matthew 2.1–12	MP Psalms **132**, 113 Jeremiah 31.7–14 John 1.29–34	EP Psalms **98**, 100 Baruch 4.36—end of 5 *or* Isaiah 60.1–9 John 2.1–11
			Holy Communion	**Morning Prayer**	**Evening Prayer**
Thursday	**7 January**	W	1 John 3.22—4.6 Psalm 2.7–end Matthew 4.12–17, 23–end	Psalms 99, **147**.1–12 *or* **78.1–39*** Isaiah 63.7–end 1 John 3	Psalms **118** *or* **78.40–end*** Baruch 1.15—2.10 *or* Jeremiah 23.1–8 Matthew 20.1–16
Friday	**8 January**	W	1 John 4.7–10 Psalm 72.1–8 Mark 6.34–44	Psalms **46**, 147.13–end *or* **55** Isaiah 64 1 John 4.7–end	Psalms 145 *or* **69** Baruch 2.11–end *or* Jeremiah 30.1–17 Matthew 20.17–28
Saturday	**9 January**	W	1 John 4.11–18 Psalm 72.1, 10–13 Mark 6.45–52	Psalms 2, **148** *or* 76, 79 Isaiah 65.1–16 1 John 5.1–12	**1st EP of the Baptism of Christ** Psalm 36; Isaiah 61 Titus 2.11–14; 3.4–7

Epiphany

If the Epiphany is celebrated on Sunday 3 January:

		Holy Communion	Morning Prayer	Evening Prayer
Saturday 2 January Basil the Great and Gregory of Nazianzus, bishops, teachers of the faith, 379 and 389 (see p.82) *Seraphim, monk, spiritual guide, 1833* *Vedanayagam Samuel Azariah, bishop, evangelist, 1945*	W	1 John 2.22–28 Psalm 98.1–4 John 1.19–28	Psalm 18.1–30 Isaiah 60.1–12 John 1.35–42	**1st EP of the Epiphany** Psalms 96, **97** Isaiah 49.1–13 John 4.7–26

		Principal Service	3rd Service	2nd Service
Sunday 3 January **Epiphany**	Gold or W	Isaiah 60.1–6 Psalm 72.[1–9] 10–15 Ephesians 3.1–12 Matthew 2.1–12	MP Psalms **132**, 113 Jeremiah 31.7–14 John 1.29–34	EP Psalms **98**, 100 Baruch 4.36—end of 5 or Isaiah 60.1–9 John 2.1–11

		Holy Communion	Morning Prayer	Evening Prayer
Monday 4 January	W	1 John 3.22—4.6 Psalm 2.7–end Matthew 4.12–17, 23–end	Psalm 89.1–37 or **71** Isaiah 60.13–end John 1.43–end	Psalms 85, **87** or **72**.75 Ruth 2 Colossians 3.1–11
Tuesday 5 January	W	1 John 4.7–10 Psalm 72.1–8 Mark 6.34–44	Psalms 8, **48** or **73** Isaiah 61 John 2.1–12	Psalms 96, **97** or **74** Ruth 3 Colossians 3.12—4.1
Wednesday 6 January	W	1 John 4.11–18 Psalm 72.1, 10–13 Mark 6.45–52	Psalms 127, 128, 131 or **77** Isaiah 62 John 2.13–end	Psalms **2**, 110 or 119.**81–104** Ruth 4.1–17 Colossians 4.2–end
Thursday 7 January	W	1 John 4.19—5.4 Psalm 72.1, 17–end Luke 4.14–22	Psalms 99, 147.1–12 or 78.**1–39*** Isaiah 63.7–end 1 John 3	Psalm 118 or 78.**40–end*** Baruch 1.15—2.10 or Jeremiah 23.1–8 Matthew 20.1–16
Friday 8 January	W	1 John 5.5–13 Psalm 147.13–end Luke 5.12–16	Psalms **46**, 147.13–end or **55** Isaiah 64 1 John 4.7–end	Psalm 145 or **69** Baruch 2.11–end or Jeremiah 30.1–17 Matthew 20.17–28
Saturday 9 January	W	1 John 5.14–end Psalm 149.1–5 John 3.22–30	Psalms **2**, 148 or 76.**79** Isaiah 65.1–16 1 John 5.1–12	**1st EP of the Baptism of Christ** Psalm 36 Isaiah 61 Titus 2.11–14; 3.4–7

Baptism of Christ (Epiphany 1)

			Principal Service	3rd Service	2nd Service
Sunday	10 January Baptism of Christ 1st Sunday of Epiphany	W	Genesis 1.1–5 Psalm 29 Acts 19.1–7 Mark 1.4–11	Psalm 89.19–29 1 Samuel 16.1–3,13 John 1.29–34	Psalms 46 [47] Isaiah 42.1–9 Ephesians 2.1–10 HC Matthew 3.13–end
			Holy Communion	**Morning Prayer**	**Evening Prayer**
Monday	11 January Mary Slessor, missionary, 1915 DEL week 1	W	Hebrews 1.1–6 Psalm 97.1–2, 6–10 Mark 1.14–20	Psalms 2, 110 or 80, 82 Amos 1 1 Corinthians 1.1–17	Psalms 34, 36 or 85, 86 Genesis 1.1–19 Matthew 21.1–17
Tuesday	12 January Aelred, abbot, 1167 (see p.84) Benedict Biscop, scholar, 689	W	Hebrews 2.5–12 Psalm 8 Mark 1.21–28	Psalms 8, 9 or 87, 89.1–18 Amos 2 1 Corinthians 1.18–end	Psalms 45, 46 or 89.19–end Genesis 1.20—2.3 Matthew 21.18–32
Wednesday	13 January Hilary, bishop, teacher of the faith, 367 Kentigern (Mungo), missionary bishop, 603 (see p.82) George Fox, founder of the Society of Friends (Quakers), 1691	W	Hebrews 2.14–end Psalm 105.1–9 Mark 1.29–39	Psalms 19, 20 or 119.105–128 Amos 3 1 Corinthians 2	Psalms 47, 48 or 91, 93 Genesis 2.4–end Matthew 21.33–end
Thursday	14 January	W	Hebrews 3.7–14 Psalm 95.1, 8–end Mark 1.40–end	Psalms 21, 24 or 90, 92 Amos 4 1 Corinthians 3	Psalms 61, 65 or 94 Genesis 3 Matthew 22.1–14
Friday	15 January	W	Hebrews 4.1–5, 11 Psalm 78.3–8 Mark 2.1–12	Psalms 67, 72 or 88, (95) Amos 5.1–17 1 Corinthians 4	Psalm 68 or 102 Genesis 4.1–16, 25–26 Matthew 22.15–33
Saturday	16 January	W	Hebrews 4.12–end Psalm 19.7–end Mark 2.13–17	Psalms 29, 33 or 96, 97, 100 Amos 5.18–end 1 Corinthians 5	Psalms 84, 85 or 104 Genesis 6.1–10 Matthew 22.34–end

Epiphany 2

		Principal Service	3rd Service	2nd Service
Sunday	17 January W 2nd Sunday of Epiphany	1 Samuel 3.1–10 [11–20] Psalm 139.1–5, 12–18 [or 139.1–9] Revelation 5.1–10 John 1.43–end	Psalm 145.1–12 Isaiah 62.1–5 1 Corinthians 6.11–end	Psalm 96 Isaiah 60.9–end Hebrews 6.17—7.10 HC Matthew 8.5–13
		Holy Communion	**Morning Prayer**	**Evening Prayer**
Monday	18 January W Week of Prayer for Christian Unity: 18–25 January Amy Carmichael, spiritual writer, 1951 DEL week 2	Hebrews 5.1–10 Psalm 110.1–4 Mark 2.18–22	Psalms 145, **146** or **98**, 99, 101 Amos 6 1 Corinthians 6.1–11	Psalm **71** or **105*** (or 103) Genesis 6.11—7.10 Matthew 24.1–14
Tuesday	19 January W Wulfstan, bishop, 1095 (see p.83)	Hebrews 6.10–end Psalm 111 Mark 2.23–end	Psalms **132**, 147.1–12 or **106*** (or 103) Amos 7 1 Corinthians 6.12–end	Psalm **89.1–37** or **107*** Genesis 7.11–end Matthew 24.15–28
Wednesday	20 January W Richard Rolle, spiritual writer, 1349	Hebrews 7.1–3, 15–17 Psalm 110.1–4 Mark 3.1–6	Psalms 81, 147.13–end or 110, **111**, 112 Amos 8 1 Corinthians 7.1–24	Psalms 97, 98 or **119.129–152** Genesis 8.1–14 Matthew 24.29–end
Thursday	21 January Wr Agnes, child martyr, 304 (see p.81)	Hebrews 7.25—8.6 Psalm 40.7–10, 17–end Mark 3.7–12	Psalms 76, 148 or 113, **115** Amos 9 1 Corinthians 7.25–end	Psalms 99, 100, **111** or 114, **116**, 117 Genesis 8.15—9.7 Matthew 25.1–13
Friday	22 January W Vincent of Saragossa, deacon, martyr, 304	Hebrews 8.6–end Psalm 85.7–end Mark 3.13–19	Psalms **27**, 149 or **139** Hosea 1.1—2.1 1 Corinthians 8	Psalm 73 or **130**, 131, 137 Genesis 9.8–19 Matthew 25.14–30
Saturday	23 January W	Hebrews 9.2–3, 11–14 Psalm 47.1–8 Mark 3.20–21	Psalms **122**, 128, 150 or 120, **121**, 122 Hosea 2.2–17 1 Corinthians 9.1–14	Psalms **61**, 66 or **118** Genesis 11.1–9 Matthew 25.31–end

Epiphany 3

		Principal Service	3rd Service	2nd Service
Sunday	**24 January** W **3rd Sunday of Epiphany**	Genesis 14.17–20 Psalm 128 Revelation 19.6–10 John 2.1–11	Psalm 113 Jonah 3.1–5, 10 John 3.16–21	Psalm 33 [or 33.1–12] Jeremiah 3.21—4.2 Titus 2.1–8, 11–14 HC Matthew 4.12–23 or: 1st EP of the Conversion of Paul: Psalm 149; Isaiah 49.1–13; Acts 22.3–16
Monday	**25 January** W Conversion of Paul	Jeremiah 1.4–10 or Acts 9.1–22 Psalm 67 Acts 9.1–22 or Galatians 1.11–16a Matthew 19.27–end	MP Psalm 66, 147.13–end Ezekiel 3.22–end Philippians 3.1–14	EP Psalm 119.41–56 Ecclesiasticus 39.1–10 or Isaiah 56.1–8 Colossians 1.24—2.7
		Holy Communion	**Morning Prayer**	**Evening Prayer**
Tuesday	**26 January** W Timothy and Titus, companions of Paul DEL week 3	Hebrews 10.1–10 Psalm 40.1–10 Mark 3.31–end *Lesser Festival eucharistic lectionary:* Isaiah 61.1–3a Psalm 100 2 Timothy 2.1–8 or Titus 1.1–5 Luke 10.1–9	Psalms 34, 36 or 132, 133 Hosea 4.1–16 1 Corinthians 10.1–13	Psalm 145 or (134), 135 Genesis 13.2–end Matthew 26.17–35
Wednesday	**27 January** W	Hebrews 10.11–18 Psalm 110.1–4 Mark 4.1–20	Psalms 45, 46 or 119.153–end Hosea 5.1–7 1 Corinthians 10.14—11.1	Psalms 21, 29 or 136 Genesis 14 Matthew 26.36–46
Thursday	**28 January** W Thomas Aquinas, priest, philosopher, teacher of the faith, 1274 (see p.82)	Hebrews 10.19–25 Psalm 24.1–6 Mark 4.21–25	Psalms 47, 48 or 143, 146 Hosea 5.8—6.6 1 Corinthians 11.2–16	Psalms 24, 33 or 138, 140, 141 Genesis 15 Matthew 26.47–56
Friday	**29 January** W	Hebrews 10.32–end Psalm 37.3–6, 40–end Mark 4.26–34	Psalms 61, 65 or 142, 144 Hosea 6.7—7.2 1 Corinthians 11.17–end	Psalms 67, 77 or 145 Genesis 16 Matthew 26.57–end

Epiphany 4 / Presentation

If the Presentation of Christ is celebrated on Tuesday 2 February:

			Holy Communion	Morning Prayer	Evening Prayer
Saturday	**30 January** Charles, king and martyr, 1649 (see p.81)	Wr	Hebrews 11.1–2, 8–19 Canticle: Luke 1.69–73 Mark 4.35–end	Psalm **68** or **147** Hosea 8 1 Corinthians 12.1–11	Psalms **72**, 76 or **148**, 149, 150 Genesis 17.1–22 Matthew 27.1–10
			Principal Service	**3rd Service**	**2nd Service**
Sunday	**31 January** 4th Sunday of Epiphany	W	Deuteronomy 18.15–20 Psalm 111 Revelation 12.1–5a Mark 1.21–28	Psalm 71.1–6, 15–17 Jeremiah 1.4–10 Mark 1.40–end	Psalm 34 [or 34.1–10] 1 Samuel 3.1–20 1 Corinthians 14.12–20 HC Matthew 13.10–17
			Holy Communion	**Morning Prayer**	**Evening Prayer**
Monday	**1 February** Brigid, abbess, c.525 DEL week 4	W	Hebrews 11.32–end Psalm 31.19–end Mark 5.1–20	Psalms **57**, 96 or 1, 2, 3 Hosea 9 1 Corinthians 12.12–end	1st **EP of the Presentation** Psalm 118 1 Samuel 1.19b–end Hebrews 4.11–end
			Principal Service	**3rd Service**	**2nd Service**
Tuesday	**2 February** **Presentation of Christ in the Temple** (Candlemas)	Gold or W	Malachi 3.1–5 Psalm 24.[1–6] 7–end Hebrews 2.14–end Luke 2.22–40	MP Psalms **48**, 146 Exodus 13.1–16 Romans 12.1–5	EP Psalms 122, **132** Haggai 2.1–9 John 2.18–22
			Holy Communion	**Morning Prayer**	**Evening Prayer**
Wednesday	**3 February** Anskar, archbishop, missionary, 865 (see p.84) Ordinary Time begins today. The Collect of 5 before Lent is used.	Gw	Hebrews 12.4–7, 11–15 Psalm 103.1–2, 13–18 Mark 6.1–6	Psalm **119**.1–32 Hosea 11.1–11 1 Corinthians 14.1–19	Psalms **11**, 12, 13 Genesis 19.1–3, 12–29 Matthew 27.45–56
Thursday	**4 February** Gilbert, founder of the Gilbertine Order, 1189	G	Hebrews 12.18–19, 21–24 Psalm 48.1–3, 8–10 Mark 6.7–13	Psalms 14, **15**, 16 Hosea 11.12—end of 12 1 Corinthians 14.20–end	Psalm **18*** Genesis 21.1–21 Matthew 27.57–end
Friday	**5 February**	G	Hebrews 13.1–8 Psalm 27.1–6, 9–12 Mark 6.14–29	Psalms 17, **19** Hosea 13.1–14 1 Corinthians 16.1–9	Psalm **22** Genesis 22.1–19 Matthew 28.1–15
Saturday	**6 February** Martyrs of Japan, 1597	G	Hebrews 13.15–17, 20–21 Psalm 23 Mark 6.30–34	Psalms 20, 21, **23** Hosea 14 1 Corinthians 16.10–end	Psalm **24**, 25 Genesis 23 Matthew 28.16–end

Presentation / Epiphany 4

If the Presentation of Christ is transferred to Sunday 31 January:

		Holy Communion	Morning Prayer	Evening Prayer
Saturday	**30 January** Wr Charles, king and martyr, 1649 (see p.81)	Hebrews 11.1–2, 8–19 Canticle: Luke 1.69–73 Mark 4.35–end	Psalm **68** or **147** Hosea 8 1 Corinthians 12.1–11	**1st EP of the Presentation** Psalm 118 1 Samuel 1.19b–end Hebrews 4.11–end
		Principal Service	**3rd Service**	**2nd Service**
Sunday	**31 January** Gold or W **Presentation of Christ in the Temple** (Candlemas)	Malachi 3.1–5 Psalm 24. [1–6] 7–end Hebrews 2.14–end Luke 2.22–40	MP Psalms **48**, **146** Exodus 13.1–16 Romans 12.1–5	EP Psalms 122, **132** Haggai 2.1–9 John 2.18–22
		Holy Communion	**Morning Prayer**	**Evening Prayer**
Monday	**1 February** G Brigid, abbess, c.525 DEL week 4 Ordinary Time begins today. The Collect of 5 before Lent is used.	Hebrews 11.32–end Psalm 31.19–end Mark 5.1–20	Psalms 1, 2, 3 Hosea 9 1 Corinthians 12.12–end	Psalms **4**, 7 Genesis 18.1–15 Matthew 27.11–26
Tuesday	**2 February** G	Hebrews 12.1–4 Psalm 22.25b–end Mark 5.21–end	Psalms **5**, 6, (8) Hosea 10 1 Corinthians 13	Psalms **9**, 10* Genesis 18.16–end Matthew 27.27–44
Wednesday	**3 February** Gw Anskar, archbishop, missionary, 865 (see p.84)	Hebrews 12.4–7, 11–15 Psalm 103.1–2, 13–18 Mark 6.1–6	Psalm **119**.1–32 Hosea 11.1–11 1 Corinthians 14.1–19	Psalms **11**, 12, 13 Genesis 19.1–3, 12–29 Matthew 27.45–56
Thursday	**4 February** G Gilbert, founder of the Gilbertine Order, 1189	Hebrews 12.18–19, 21–24 Psalm 48.1–3, 8–10 Mark 6.7–13	Psalms 14, **15**, 16 Hosea 11.12–end of 12 1 Corinthians 14.20–end	Psalm 18* Genesis 21.1–21 Matthew 27.57–end
Friday	**5 February** G	Hebrews 13.1–8 Psalm 27.1–6, 9–12 Mark 6.14–29	Psalms 17, **19** Hosea 13.1–14 1 Corinthians 16.1–9	Psalm **22** Genesis 22.1–19 Matthew 28.1–15
Saturday	**6 February** G Martyrs of Japan, 1597	Hebrews 13.15–17, 20–21 Psalm 23 Mark 6.30–34	Psalms 20, 21, **23** Hosea 14 1 Corinthians 16.10–end	Psalm **24**, 25 Genesis 23 Matthew 28.16–end

Sunday next before Lent

			Principal Service	3rd Service	2nd Service
Sunday	7 February Sunday next before Lent	G	2 Kings 2.1–12 Psalm 50.1–6 2 Corinthians 4.3–6 Mark 9.2–9	Psalms 27, 150 Exodus 24.12–end 2 Corinthians 3.12–end	Psalms 2 [99] 1 Kings 19.1–16 2 Peter 1.16–end HC Mark 9.[2–8] 9–13
			Holy Communion	**Morning Prayer**	**Evening Prayer**
Monday	8 February DEL week 5	G	Genesis 1.1–19 Psalm 104.1, 2, 6–13, 26 Mark 6.53–end	Psalms 27, **30** Jeremiah 1 John 3.1–21	Psalms 26, **28, 29** Genesis 37.1–11 Galatians 1
Tuesday	9 February	G	Genesis 1.20—2.4a Psalm 8 Mark 7.1–13	Psalms 32, **36** Jeremiah 2.1–13 John 3.22–end	Psalm **33** Genesis 37.12–end Galatians 2.1–10
			Principal Service	**3rd Service**	**2nd Service**
Wednesday	10 February Ash Wednesday	P(La)	Joel 2.1–2, 12–17 or Isaiah 58.1–12 Psalm 51.1–18 2 Corinthians 5.20b—6.10 Matthew 6.1–6, 16–21 or John 8.1–11	MP Psalm **38** Daniel 9.3–6, 17–19 1 Timothy 6.6–19	EP Psalm **51** or 102 [or 102.1–18] Isaiah 1.10–18 Luke 15.11–end
			Holy Communion	**Morning Prayer**	**Evening Prayer**
Thursday	11 February	P(La)	Deuteronomy 30.15–end Psalm 1 Luke 9.22–25	Psalm **77** or **37*** Jeremiah 2.14–32 John 4.1–26	Psalm 74 or 39, **40** Genesis 39 Galatians 2.11–end
Friday	12 February	P(La)	Isaiah 58.1–9a Psalm 51.1–5, 17–18 Matthew 9.14–15	Psalms **3**, 7 or **31** Jeremiah 3.6–22 John 4.27–42	Psalm **31** or **35** Genesis 40 Galatians 3.1–14
Saturday	13 February	P(La)	Isaiah 58.9b–end Psalm **86**.1–7 Luke 5.27–32	Psalm 71 or 41, **42**, 43 Jeremiah 4.1–18 John 4.43–end	Psalm 73 or 45, **46** Genesis 41.1–24 Galatians 3.15–22

Lent 1

		Principal Service	3rd Service	2nd Service
Sunday	**14 February** *P(La)* **1st Sunday of Lent**	Genesis 9.8–17 Psalm 25.1–9 1 Peter 3.18–end Mark 1.9–15	Psalm 77 Exodus 34.1–10 Romans 10.8b–13	Psalm 119.17–32 Genesis 2.15–17; 3.1–7 Romans 5.12–19 H/C Luke 13.31–end
		Holy Communion	**Morning Prayer**	**Evening Prayer**
Monday	**15 February** *P(La)* Sigfrid, bishop, 1045 Thomas Bray, priest, *founder of SPCK and SPG, 1730*	Leviticus 19.1–2, 11–18 Psalm 19.7–end Matthew 25.31–end	Psalms 10, 11 or **44** Jeremiah 4.19–end John 5.1–18	Psalms 12, **13**, 14 or **47**, 49 Genesis 41.25–45 Galatians 3.23—4.7
Tuesday	**16 February** *P(La)*	Isaiah 55.10–11 Psalm 34.4–6, 21–22 Matthew 6.7–15	Psalms **44** or **48**, 52 Jeremiah 5.1–19 John 5.19–29	Psalms 46, **49** or **50** Genesis 41.46—42.5 Galatians 4.8–20
Wednesday	**17 February** *P(La)r* Janani Luwum, archbishop, martyr, 1977 (see p.81) Ember Day	Jonah 3 Psalm 51.1–5, 17–18 Luke 11.29–32	Psalms **6**, 17 or 119.**57–80** Jeremiah 5.20–end John 5.30–end	Psalms 9, **28** or **59**, 60, (67) Genesis 42.6–17 Galatians 4.21—5.1
Thursday	**18 February** *P(La)*	Esther 14.1–5, 12–14 or Isaiah 55.6–9 Psalm 138 Matthew 7.7–12	Psalms **42**, 43 or 56, **57**, (63*) Jeremiah 6.9–21 John 6.1–15	Psalms 137, 138, **142** or 61, **62**, 64 Genesis 42.18–28 Galatians 5.2–15
Friday	**19 February** *P(La)* Ember Day	Ezekiel 18.21–28 Psalm 130 Matthew 5.20–26	Psalm **22** or 51, **54** Jeremiah 6.22–end John 6.16–27	Psalms 54, **55** or **38** Genesis 42.29–end Galatians 5.16–end
Saturday	**20 February** *P(La)* Ember Day	Deuteronomy 26.16–end Psalm 119.1–8 Matthew 5.43–end	Psalms 59, **63** or **68** Jeremiah 7.1–20 John 6.27–40	Psalms 4, 16 or 65, **66** Genesis 43.1–15 Galatians 6

Lent 2

			Principal Service	3rd Service	2nd Service
Sunday	21 February 2nd Sunday of Lent	P(La)	Genesis 17.1–7, 15, 16 Psalm 22.23–end Romans 4.13–end Mark 8.31–end	Psalm 105.1–6, 37–end Isaiah 51.1–11 Galatians 3.1–9, 23–end	Psalm 135 [or 135.1–14] Genesis 12.1–9 Hebrews 11.1–3, 8–16 HC John 8.51–end
			Holy Communion	**Morning Prayer**	**Evening Prayer**
Monday	22 February	P(La)	Daniel 9.4–10 Psalm 79.8–9, 12, 14 Luke 6.36–38	Psalms 26, 32 or 71 Jeremiah 7.21–end John 6.41–51	Psalms 70, 74 or 72, 75 Genesis 43.16–end Hebrews 1
Tuesday	23 February Polycarp, bishop, martyr, c.155 (see p.81)	P(La)r	Isaiah 1.10, 16–20 Psalm 50.8, 16–end Matthew 23.1–12	Psalm 50 or 73 Jeremiah 8.1–15 John 6.52–59	Psalms 52, 53, 54 or 74 Genesis 44.1–17 Hebrews 2.1–9
Wednesday	24 February	P(La)	Jeremiah 18.18–20 Psalm 31.4–5, 14–18 Matthew 20.17–28	Psalm 35 or 77 Jeremiah 8.18—9.11 John 6.60–end	Psalms 3, 51 or 119.81–104 Genesis 44.18–end Hebrews 2.10–end
Thursday	25 February	P(La)	Jeremiah 17.5–10 Psalm 1 Luke 16.19–end	Psalm 34 or 78.1–39* Jeremiah 9.12–24 John 7.1–13	Psalm 71 or 78.40–end* Genesis 45.1–15 Hebrews 3.1–6
Friday	26 February	P(La)	Genesis 37.3–4, 12–13, 17–28 Psalm 105.16–22 Matthew 21.33–43, 45–46	Psalms 40, 41 or 55 Jeremiah 10.1–16 John 7.14–24	Psalms 6, 38 or 69 Genesis 45.16–end Hebrews 3.7–end
Saturday	27 February George Herbert, priest, poet, 1633 (see p.83)	P(La)w	Micah 7.14–15, 18–20 Psalm 103.1–4, 9–12 Luke 15.1–3, 11–end	Psalms 3, 25 or 76, 79 Jeremiah 10.17–24 John 7.25–36	Psalms 23, 27 or 81, 84 Genesis 46.1–7, 28–end Hebrews 4.1–13

Lent 3

			Principal Service	3rd Service	2nd Service
Sunday	28 February 3rd Sunday of Lent	*P(La)*	Exodus 20.1–17 Psalm 19 [or 19.7–end] 1 Corinthians 1.18–25 John 2.13–22	Psalm 18.1–25 Jeremiah 38 Philippians 1.1–26	Psalms 11, 12 Exodus 5.1—6.1 Philippians 3.4b–14 HC Matthew 10.16–22
			Holy Communion	**Morning Prayer**	**Evening Prayer**
	The following readings may replace those provided for Holy Communion on any day during the Third Week of Lent: Exodus 17.1–7; Psalm 95.1–2, 6–end; John 4.5–42				
Monday	1 March David, bishop, patron of Wales, c.601 (see p.83)	*P(La)w*	2 Kings 5.1–15 Psalms 42.1–2; 43.1–4 Luke 4.24–30	Psalms 5, 7 or 80, 82 Jeremiah 11.1–17 John 7.37–52	Psalms 11, 17 or 85, 86 Genesis 47.1–27 Hebrews 4.14—5.10
Tuesday	2 March Chad, bishop, missionary, 672 (see p.84)	*P(La)w*	Song of the Three 2, 11–20 or Daniel 2.20–23 Psalm 25.3–10 Matthew 18.21–end	Psalms 6, 9 or 87, 89.1–18 Jeremiah 11.18—12.6 John 7.53—8.11	Psalms 61, 62, 64 or 89.19–end Genesis 47.28–end of 48 Hebrews 5.11—6.12
Wednesday	3 March	*P(La)*	Deuteronomy 4.1, 5–9 Psalm 147.13–end Matthew 5.17–19	Psalm 38 or 119.105–128 Jeremiah 13.1–11 John 8.12–30	Psalms 36.39 or 91, 93 Genesis 49.1–32 Hebrews 6.13–end
Thursday	4 March	*P(La)*	Jeremiah 7.23–28 Psalm 95.1–2, 6–end Luke 11.14–23	Psalms 56, 57 or 90, 92 Jeremiah 14 John 8.31–47	Psalms 59, 60 or 94 Genesis 49.33–end of 50 Hebrews 7.1–10
Friday	5 March	*P(La)*	Hosea 14 Psalm 81.6–10, 13, 16 Mark 12.28–34	Psalm 22 or 88, (95) Jeremiah 15.10–end John 8.48–end	Psalm 69 or 102 Exodus 1.1–14 Hebrews 7.11–end
Saturday	6 March	*P(La)*	Hosea 5.15—6.6 Psalm 51.1–2, 17–end Luke 18.9–14	Psalm 31 or 96, 97, 100 Jeremiah 16.10—17.4 John 9.1–17	Psalms 116, 130 or 104 Exodus 1.22—2.10 Hebrews 8

Lent 4

			Principal Service	3rd Service	2nd Service
Sunday	7 March 4th Sunday of Lent	P(La)	Numbers 21.4–9 Psalm 107.1–3, 17–22 [or 107.1–9] Ephesians 2.1–10 John 3.14–21	Psalm 27 1 Samuel 16.1–13 John 9.1–25	Psalms 13, 14 Exodus 6.2–13 Romans 5.1–11 HC John 12.1–8

For Mothering Sunday:
Exodus 2.1–10 or 1 Samuel 1.20–end; Psalm 34.11–20 or Psalm 127.1–4; 2 Corinthians 1.3–7 or Colossians 3.12–17; Luke 2.33–35 or John 19.25b–27
If the Principal Service readings have been displaced by Mothering Sunday provisions, they may be used at the Second Service.

			Holy Communion	Morning Prayer	Evening Prayer
			The following readings may replace those provided for Holy Communion on any day during the Fourth Week of Lent: Micah 7.7–9; Psalm 27.1, 9–10, 16–17; John 9		
Monday	8 March Edward King, bishop, 1910 (see p.83) Felix, bishop, 647 Geoffrey Studdert Kennedy, priest, poet, 1929	P(La)w	Isaiah 65.17–21 Psalm 30.1–5, 8, 11–end John 4.43–end	Psalms 70, 77 or 98, 99, 101 Jeremiah 17.5–18 John 9.18–end	Psalms 25, 28 or 105* (or 103) Exodus 2.11–22 Hebrews 9.1–14
Tuesday	9 March	P(La)	Ezekiel 47.1–9, 12 Psalm 46.1–8 John 5.1–3, 5–16	Psalms 54, 79 or 106* (or 103) Jeremiah 18.1–12 John 10.1–10	Psalms 80, 82 or 107* Exodus 2.23–3.20 Hebrews 9.15–end
Wednesday	10 March	P(La)	Isaiah 49.8–15 Psalm 145.8–18 John 5.17–30	Psalms 63, 90 or 110, 111, 112 Jeremiah 18.13–end John 10.11–21	Psalms 52, 91 or 119.129–152 Exodus 4.1–23 Hebrews 10.1–18
Thursday	11 March	P(La)	Exodus 32.7–14 Psalm 106.19–23 John 5.31–end	Psalms 53, 86 or 113, 115 Jeremiah 19.1–13 John 10.22–end	Psalms 94 or 114, 116, 117 Exodus 4.27–6.1 Hebrews 10.19–25
Friday	12 March	P(La)	Wisdom 2.1, 12–22 or Jeremiah 26.8–11 Psalm 34.15–end John 7.1–2, 10, 25–30	Psalm 102 or 139 Jeremiah 19.14–20.6 John 11.1–16	Psalms 13, 16 or 130, 131, 137 Exodus 6.2–13 Hebrews 10.26–end
Saturday	13 March	P(La)	Jeremiah 11.18–20 Psalm 7.1–2, 8–10 John 7.40–52	Psalm 32 or 120, 121, 122 Jeremiah 20.7–end John 11.17–27	Psalms 140, 141, 142 or 118 Exodus 7.8–end Hebrews 11.1–16

Lent 5

		Principal Service	3rd Service	2nd Service
Sunday	**14 March** P(La) **5th Sunday of Lent** *Passiontide begins*	Jeremiah 31.31–34 Psalm 51.1–13 or Psalm 119.9–16 Hebrews 5.5–10 John 12.20–33	Psalm 107.1–22 Exodus 24.3–8 Hebrews 12.18–end	Psalm 34 [or 34.1–10] Exodus 7.8–24 Romans 5.12–end HC Luke 22.1–13
		Holy Communion	**Morning Prayer**	**Evening Prayer**

The following readings may replace those provided for Holy Communion on any day during the Fifth Week of Lent (except the Festival of Joseph of Nazareth):
2 Kings 4.18–21, 32–37; Psalm 17.1–8, 16; John 11.1–45

Monday	**15 March** P(La)	Susannah 1–9, 15–17, 19–30, 33–62 [or 41b–62] or Joshua 2.1–14 Psalm 23 John 8.1–11	Psalms **73**, 121 or 123, 124, 125, **126** Jeremiah 21.1–10 John 11.28–44	Psalms **26**, 27 or **127**, 128, 129 Exodus 8.1–19 Hebrews 11.17–31
Tuesday	**16 March** P(La)	Numbers 21.4–9 Psalm 102.1–3, 16–23 John 8.21–30	Psalms **35**, 123 or **132**, 133 Jeremiah 22.1–5, 13–19 John 11.45–end	Psalms **61**, 64 or (134), **135** Exodus 8.20–end Hebrews 11.32—12.2
Wednesday	**17 March** P(La)w Patrick, bishop, missionary, patron of Ireland, c.460 (see p.84)	Daniel 3.14–20, 24–25, 28 *Canticle:* Bless the Lord John 8.31–42	Psalms **55**, 124 or **119**.153–end Jeremiah 22.20—23.8 John 12.1–11	Psalms 56, **62** or **136** Exodus 9.1–12 Hebrews 12.3–13
Thursday	**18 March** P(La) *Cyril, bishop, teacher of the faith, 386*	Genesis 17.3–9 Psalm 105.4–9 John 8.51–end	Psalms 40, **125** or **143**, 146 Jeremiah 23.9–32 John 12.12–19	Psalms 42, **43** or **138**, 140, 141 Exodus 9.13–end Hebrews 12.14–end or: 1st EP of Joseph of Nazareth: Psalm 132; Hosea 11.1–9; Luke 2.41–end
		Principal Service	**3rd Service**	**2nd Service**
Friday	**19 March** W Joseph of Nazareth	2 Samuel 7.4–16 Psalm 89.26–36 Romans 4.13–18 Matthew 1.18–end	MP Psalms 25, 147.1–12 Isaiah 11.1–10 Matthew 13.54–end	EP Psalms 1, 112 Genesis 50.22–end Matthew 2.13–end
		Holy Communion	**Morning Prayer**	**Evening Prayer**
Saturday	**20 March** P(La)w Cuthbert, bishop, missionary, 687 (see p.84)	Ezekiel 37.21–end *Canticle:* Jeremiah 31.10–13 or Psalm 121 John 11.45–end	Psalms **23**, 127 or **147** Jeremiah 25.1–14 John 12.36b–end	Psalms 128, 129, **130** or **148**, 149, 150 Exodus 11 Hebrews 13.17–end

Holy Week

		Principal Service	3rd Service	2nd Service
Sunday 21 March **Palm Sunday**	R	*Liturgy of the Palms:* Mark 11.1–11 *or* John 12.12–16 Psalm 118.1–2, 19–end [*or* 118.19–24] *Liturgy of the Passion:* Isaiah 50.4–9a Psalm 31.9–16 [*or* 31.9–18] Philippians 2.5–11 Mark 14.1—end of 15 *or* Mark 15.1–39 [40–end]	Psalms 61, 62 Zechariah 9.9–12 1 Corinthians 2.1–12	Psalm 69.1–20 Isaiah 5.1–7 Mark 12.1–12

		Holy Communion	Morning Prayer	Evening Prayer
			From the Monday of Holy Week until the Saturday of Easter Week the seasonal psalmody must be used.	
Monday 22 March Monday of Holy Week	R	Isaiah 42.1–9 Psalm 36.5–11 Hebrews 9.11–15 John 12.1–11	Psalm 41 Lamentations 1.1–12a Luke 22.1–23	Psalm 25 Lamentations 2.8–19 Colossians 1.18–23
Tuesday 23 March Tuesday of Holy Week	R	Isaiah 49.1–7 Psalm 71.1–14 [*or* 71.1–8] 1 Corinthians 1.18–31 John 12.20–36	Psalm 27 Lamentations 3.1–18 Luke 22. [24–38] 39–53	Psalm 55.13–24 Lamentations 3.40–51 Galatians 6.11–end
Wednesday 24 March Wednesday of Holy Week	R	Isaiah 50.4–9a Psalm 70 Hebrews 12.1–3 John 13.21–32	Psalm 102 [*or* 102.1–18] Wisdom 1.16—2.1; 2.12–22 *or* Jeremiah 11.18–20 Luke 22.54–end	Psalm 88 Isaiah 63.1–9 Revelation 14.18—15.4
Thursday 25 March **Maundy Thursday**	W	Exodus 12.1–4 [5–10] 11–14 Psalm 116.1, 10–end [*or* 116.9–end] 1 Corinthians 11.23–26 John 13.1–17, 31b–35	Psalms 42, 43 Leviticus 16.2–24 Luke 23.1–25	Psalm 39 Exodus 11 Ephesians 2.11–18
Friday 26 March **Good Friday**	Hangings removed; R for the Liturgy	Isaiah 52.13—end of 53 Psalm 22 [*or* 22.1–11 *or* 22.1–21] Hebrews 10.16–25 *or* Hebrews 4.14–16; 5.7–9 John 18.1—end of 19	Psalm 69 Genesis 22.1–18 *A part of John 18 and 19 may be read, if not used at the Principal Service* *or* Hebrews 10.1–10	Psalms 130, 143 Lamentations 5.15–end John 19.38–end *or* Colossians 1.18–23

Easter

		Principal Service	3rd Service	2nd Service
Saturday	**27 March** **Easter Eve** *Hangings removed* These readings are for use at services other than the Easter Vigil.	Job 14.1–14 or Lamentations 3.1–9, 19–24 Psalm 31.1–4, 15–16 [or 31.1–5] 1 Peter 4.1–8 Matthew 27.57–end or John 19.38–end	Psalm 142 Hosea 6.1–6 John 2.18–22	Psalm 116 Job 19.21–27 1 John 5.5–12

Vigil Readings

Complementary Psalmody

Saturday or Sunday	**27 March evening** **28 March morning** *Easter Vigil* *Gold or W* The New Testament readings should be preceded by a minimum of three Old Testament readings. The Exodus reading should always be used.	Genesis 1.1—2.4a Genesis 7.1–5, 11–18; 8.6–18; 9.8–13 Genesis 22.1–18 **Exodus 14.10–end; 15.20–21** Isaiah 55.1–11 Baruch 3.9–15, 32—4.4 or Proverbs 8.1–8, 19–21; 9.4b–6 Ezekiel 36.24–28 Ezekiel 37.1–14 Zephaniah 3.14–end **Romans 6.3–11** **Mark 16.1–8**	Psalm 136.1–9, 23–end Psalm 46 Psalm 16 *Canticle:* Exodus 15.1b–13, 17–18 *Canticle:* Isaiah 12.2–end Psalm 19 Psalms 42, 43 Psalm 143 Psalm 98 **Psalm 114**	

		Principal Service	3rd Service	2nd Service
Sunday	**28 March** **Easter Day** *Gold or W*	Acts 10.34–43 † or Isaiah 25.6–9 Psalm 118.1–2, 14–24 [or 118.14–24] 1 Corinthians 15.1–11 or Acts 10.34–43† John 20.1–18 or Mark 16.1–8 † *The reading from Acts must be used as either the first or second reading.*	MP Psalms 114, 117 Genesis 1.1–5, 26–end 2 Corinthians 5.14—6.2	EP Psalms 105 or 66.1–11 Ezekiel 37.1–14 Luke 24.13–35

Easter Week

			Holy Communion	Morning Prayer	Evening Prayer
Monday	**29 March**	W	Acts 2.14, 22–32	Psalms **111**, 117, 146	Psalm **135**
	Monday of Easter Week		Psalm 16.1–2, 6–end	Song of Solomon 1.9—2.7	Exodus 12.1–14
			Matthew 28.8–15	Mark 16.1–8	1 Corinthians 15.1–11
Tuesday	**30 March**	W	Acts 2.36–41	Psalms **112**, 147.1–12	Psalm **136**
	Tuesday of Easter Week		Psalm 33.4–5, 18–end	Song of Solomon 2.8–end	Exodus 12.14–36
			John 20.11–18	Luke 24.1–12	1 Corinthians 15.12–19
Wednesday	**31 March**	W	Acts 3.1–10	Psalms **113**, 147.13–end	Psalm **105**
	Wednesday of Easter Week		Psalm 105.1–9	Song of Solomon 3	Exodus 12.37–end
			Luke 24.13–35	Matthew 28.16–end	1 Corinthians 15.20–28
Thursday	**1 April**	W	Acts 3.11–end	Psalms **114**, 148	Psalm **106**
	Thursday of Easter Week		Psalm 8	Song of Solomon 5.2—6.3	Exodus 13.1–16
			Luke 24.35–48	Luke 7.11–17	1 Corinthians 15.29–34
Friday	**2 April**	W	Acts 4.1–12	Psalms **115**, 149	Psalm **107**
	Friday of Easter Week		Psalm 118.1–4, 22–26	Song of Solomon 7.10—8.4	Exodus 13.17—14.14
			John 21.1–14	Luke 8.41–end	1 Corinthians 15.35–50
Saturday	**3 April**	W	Acts 4.13–21	Psalms **116**, 150	Psalm **145**
	Saturday of Easter Week		Psalm 118.1–4, 14–21	Song of Solomon 8.5–7	Exodus 14.15–end
			Mark 16.9–15	John 11.17–44	1 Corinthians 15.51–end

Easter 2

		Principal Service	3rd Service	2nd Service
Sunday	**4 April** W **2nd Sunday of Easter**	[Exodus 14.10–end; 15.20, 21] Acts 4.32–35 † Psalm 133 1 John 1.1—2.2 John 20.19–end † *The reading from Acts must be used as either the first or second reading.*	Psalm 22.20–end Isaiah 53.6–12 Romans 4.13–25	**1st EP of the Annunciation** Psalm 85 Wisdom 9.1–12 or Genesis 3.8–15 Galatians 4.1–5
Monday	**5 April** Gold or W **Annunciation of Our Lord to the Blessed Virgin Mary**	Isaiah 7.10–14 Psalm 40.5–11 Hebrews 10.4–10 Luke 1.26–38	MP Psalms 111, 113 1 Samuel 2.1–10 Romans 5.12–end	EP Psalms 131, 146 Isaiah 52.1–12 Hebrews 2.5–end
		Holy Communion	**Morning Prayer**	**Evening Prayer**
Tuesday	**6 April** W	Acts 4.32–end Psalm 93 John 3.7–15	Psalms **8**, 20, 21 or **5, 6**, (8) Deuteronomy 1.19–40 John 20.11–18	Psalm **104** or **9**, 10* Exodus 15.22—16.10 Colossians 1.15–end
Wednesday	**7 April** W	Acts 5.17–26 Psalm 34.1–8 John 3.16–21	Psalms 16, **30** or **119.1–32** Deuteronomy 3.18–end John 20.19–end	Psalm **33** or **11**, 12, 13 Exodus 16.11–end Colossians 2.1–15
Thursday	**8 April** W	Acts 5.27–33 Psalm 34.1, 15–end John 3.31–end	Psalms **28**, 29 or 14, **15**, 16 Deuteronomy 4.1–14 John 21.1–14	Psalms **34** or **18*** Exodus 17 Colossians 2.16—3.11
Friday	**9 April** W Dietrich Bonhoeffer, Lutheran pastor, martyr, 1945	Acts 5.34–42 Psalm 27.1–5, 16–17 John 6.1–15	Psalms 57, **61** or 17, **19** Deuteronomy 4.15–31 John 21.15–19	Psalm 118 or **22** Exodus 18.1–12 Colossians 3.12—4.1
Saturday	**10 April** W William Law, priest, spiritual writer 1761 (see p.82) William of Ockham, friar, philosopher, teacher of the faith, 1347	Acts 6.1–7 Psalm 33.1–5, 18–19 John 6.16–21	Psalms 63, **84** or 20, 21, **23** Deuteronomy 4.32–40 John 21.20–end	Psalm **66** or 24, 25 Exodus 18.13–end Colossians 4.2–end

Easter 3

		Principal Service	3rd Service	2nd Service
Sunday	11 April 3rd Sunday of Easter W	[Zephaniah 3.14–end] Acts 3.12–19 † Psalm 4 1 John 3.1–7 Luke 24.36b–48 † *The reading from Acts must be used as either the first or second reading.*	Psalm 77.11–end Isaiah 63.7–15 1 Corinthians 10.1–13	Psalm 142 Deuteronomy 7.7–13 Revelation 2.1–11 HC Luke 16.19–end
		Holy Communion	**Morning Prayer**	**Evening Prayer**
Monday	12 April W	Acts 6.8–15 Psalm 119.17–24 John 6.22–29	Psalms **96**, 97 or 27, **30** Deuteronomy 5.1–22 Ephesians 1.1–14	Psalm **61**, 65 or 26, **28**, 29 Exodus 19 Luke 1.1–25
Tuesday	13 April W	Acts 7.51–8.1a Psalm 31.1–5, 16 John 6.30–35	Psalms **98**, 99, 100 or 32, **36** Deuteronomy 5.22–end Ephesians 1.15–end	Psalm **71** or 33 Exodus 20.1–21 Luke 1.26–38
Wednesday	14 April W	Acts 8.1b–8 Psalm 66.1–6 John 6.35–40	Psalm 105 or **34** Deuteronomy 6 Ephesians 2.1–10	Psalms 67, **72** or 119.**33–56** Exodus 24 Luke 1.39–56
Thursday	15 April W	Acts 8.26–end Psalm 66.7–8, 14–end John 6.44–51	Psalm 136 or **37*** Deuteronomy 7.1–11 Ephesians 2.11–end	Psalm **73** or 39, **40** Exodus 25.1–22 Luke 1.57–end
Friday	16 April W *Isabella Gilmore, deaconess, 1923*	Acts 9.1–20 Psalm 117 John 6.52–59	Psalm 107 or **31** Deuteronomy 7.12–end Ephesians 3.1–13	Psalm **77** or **35** Exodus 28.1–4a, 29–38 Luke 1.1–20
Saturday	17 April W	Acts 9.31–42 Psalm 116.10–15 John 6.60–69	Psalms 108, **110**, 111 or 41, **42**, 43 Deuteronomy 8 Ephesians 3.14–end	Psalms 23, **27** or 45, **46** Exodus 29.1–9 Luke 2.21–40

Easter 4

		Principal Service	3rd Service	2nd Service
Sunday	**18 April** W **4th Sunday of Easter**	[Genesis 7.1–5, 11–18; 8.6–18; 9.8–13] Acts 4.5–12 † Psalm 23 1 John 3.16–end John 10.11–18 † *The reading from Acts must be used as either the first or second reading.*	Psalm 119.89–96 Nehemiah 7.73b—8.12 Luke 24.25–32	Psalm 81.8–end Exodus 16.4–15 Revelation 2.12–17 HC John 6.30–40
		Holy Communion	**Morning Prayer**	**Evening Prayer**
Monday	**19 April** Wr Alphege, archbishop, martyr, 1012 (see p.81)	Acts 11.1–18 Psalms 42.1–2; 43.1–4 John 10.1–10 (or 11–18)	Psalm **103** or **44** Deuteronomy 9.1–21 Ephesians 4.1–16	Psalms 112, 113, **114** or **47**, **49** Exodus 32.1–14 Luke 2.41–end
Tuesday	**20 April** W	Acts 11.19–26 Psalm **87** John 10.22–30	Psalm **139**, or **48**, **52** Deuteronomy 9.23—10.5 Ephesians 4.17–end	Psalms 115, **116** or **50** Exodus 32.15–34 Luke 3.1–14
Wednesday	**21 April** W Anselm, abbot, archbishop, teacher of the faith, 1109 (see p.82)	Acts 12.24—13.5 Psalm **67** John 12.44–end	Psalm **135** or **119.57–80** Deuteronomy 10.12–end Ephesians 5.1–14	Psalms **47**, 48 or **59**, 60, (67) Exodus 33 Luke 3.15–22
Thursday	**22 April** W	Acts 13.13–25 Psalm 89.1–2, 20–26 John 13.16–20	Psalm **118** or 56, **57**, (63*) Deuteronomy 11.8–end Ephesians 5.15–end	Psalms 81, **85** or 61, **62**, **64** Exodus 34.1–10, 27–end Luke 4.1–13 *or:* 1st EP of George, martyr, patron of England: Psalms 111, 116; Jeremiah 15.15–end; Hebrews 11.32—12.2
		Principal Service	**3rd Service**	**2nd Service**
Friday	**23 April** R George, martyr, patron of England, c.304	1 Maccabees 2.59–64 *or* Revelation 12.7–12 Psalm 126 2 Timothy 2.3–13 John 15.18–21	*MP* Psalms 5, 146 Joshua 1.1–9 Ephesians 6.10–20	*EP* Psalms 3, 11 Isaiah 43.1–7 John 15.1–8
		Holy Communion	**Morning Prayer**	**Evening Prayer**
Saturday	**24 April** W Mellitus, bishop, 624 Seven Martyrs of the Melanesian Brotherhood, 2003	Acts 13.44–end Psalm 98.1–5 John 14.7–14	Psalms **34** or **68** Deuteronomy 15.1–18 Ephesians 6.10–end	Psalms **84**, 86 or 65, **66** Exodus 40.17–end Luke 4.31–37

Easter 5

		Principal Service	3rd Service	2nd Service
Sunday	**25 April** W **5th Sunday of Easter**	[Baruch 3.9–15, 32—4.4 or Genesis 22.1–18] Acts 8.26–end † Psalm 22.25–end 1 John 4.7–end John 15.1–8 † The reading from Acts must be used as either the first or second reading.	Psalm 44.16–end 2 Maccabees 7.7–14 or Daniel 3.16–28 Hebrews 11.32—12.2	Psalm 96 Isaiah 60.1–14 Revelation 3.1–13 HC Mark 16.9–16 or: 1st EP of Mark the Evangelist: Psalm 19; Isaiah 52.7–10; Mark 1.1–15
Monday	**26 April** R Mark the Evangelist (transferred from 25 April)	Proverbs 15.28–end or Acts 15.35–end Psalm 119.9–16 Ephesians 4.7–16 Mark 13.5–13	MP Psalms 37.23–end, 148 Isaiah 62.6–10 or Ecclesiasticus 51.13–end Acts 12.25—13.13	EP Psalm 45 Ezekiel 1.4–14 2 Timothy 4.1–11
		Holy Communion	**Morning Prayer**	**Evening Prayer**
Tuesday	**27 April** W Christina Rossetti, poet, 1894	Acts 14.19–end Psalm 145.10–end John 14.27–end	Psalms 19, 147.1–12 or 73 Deuteronomy 17.8–end 1 Peter 1.13–end	Psalms 96, 97 or 74 Numbers 11.1–33 Luke 5.1–11
Wednesday	**28 April** W Peter Chanel, missionary, martyr, 1841	Acts 15.1–6 Psalm 122.1–5 John 15.1–8	Psalms 30, 147.13–end or 77 Deuteronomy 18.9–end 1 Peter 2.1–10	Psalms 98, 99, 100 or 119.81–104 Numbers 12 Luke 5.12–26
Thursday	**29 April** W Catherine of Siena, teacher of the faith, 1380 (see p.82)	Acts 15.7–21 Psalm 96.1–3, 7–10 John 15.9–11	Psalms 57, 148 or 78.1–39* Deuteronomy 19 1 Peter 2.11–end	Psalms 104 or 78.40–end* Numbers 13.1–3, 17–end Luke 5.27–end
Friday	**30 April** W Pandita Mary Ramabai, translator, 1922	Acts 15.22–31 Psalm 57.8–end John 15.12–17	Psalms 138, 149 or 55 Deuteronomy 21.22—22.8 1 Peter 3.1–12	Psalm 66 or 69 Numbers 14.1–25 Luke 6.1–11 or: 1st EP of Philip and James, Apostles: Psalm 25; Isaiah 40.27–end; John 12.20–26
		Principal Service	**3rd Service**	**2nd Service**
Saturday	**1 May** R Philip and James, Apostles	Isaiah 30.15–21 Psalm 119.1–8 Ephesians 1.3–10 John 14.1–14	MP Psalms 139, 146 Proverbs 4.10–18 James 1.1–12	EP Psalm 149 Job 23.1–12 John 1.43–end

Easter 6

			Principal Service	3rd Service	2nd Service
Sunday	2 May **6th Sunday of Easter**	W	[Isaiah 55.1–11] Acts 10.44–end † Psalm 98 1 John 5.1–6 John 15.9–17 † The reading from Acts must be used as either the first or second reading.	Psalm 104.28–34 Ezekiel 47.1–12 John 21.1–19	Psalm 45 Song of Solomon 4.16—5.2; 8.6,7 Revelation 3.14–end HC Luke 22.24–30
			Holy Communion	**Morning Prayer**	**Evening Prayer**
Monday	3 May Rogation Day	W	Acts 16.11–15 Psalm 149.1–5 John 15.26—16.4	Psalms **65**, 67 or 80, 82 Deuteronomy 26 1 Peter 4.1–11	Psalms 121, 122, 123 or **85**, 86 Numbers 16.1–35 Luke 6.27–38
Tuesday	4 May English Saints and Martyrs of the Reformation Era Rogation Day	W	Acts 16.22–34 Psalm 138 John 16.5–11 *Lesser Festival eucharistic lectionary:* Isaiah 43.1–7 or Ecclesiasticus 2.10–17 Psalm 87 2 Corinthians 4.5–12 John 12.20–26	Psalms 124, 125, **126**, 127 or 87, **89.1–18** Deuteronomy 28.1–14 1 Peter 4.12–end	Psalms **128**, 129, 130, 131 or **89.19–end** Numbers 16.36–end Luke 6.39–end
Wednesday	5 May Rogation Day	W	Acts 17.15, 22—18.1 Psalm 148.1–2, 11–end John 16.12–15	Psalms **132**, 133 or **119.105–128** Deuteronomy 28.58–end 1 Peter 5	**1st EP of Ascension Day** Psalms 15, 24 2 Samuel 23.1–5 Colossians 2.20—3.4
			Principal Service	**3rd Service**	**2nd Service**
Thursday	6 May **Ascension Day**	Gold or W	Acts 1.1–11 † or Daniel 7.9–14 Psalm 47 or Psalm 93 Ephesians 1.15–end or Acts 1.1–11 † Luke 24.44–end † The reading from Acts must be used as either the first or second reading.	MP Psalms 110, 150 Isaiah 52.7–end Hebrews 7. [11–25] 26–end	EP Psalm 8 Song of the Three 29–37 or 2 Kings 2.1–15 Revelation 5 HC Matthew 28.16–end

The nine days after Ascension Day until the eve of Pentecost are observed as days of prayer and preparation for the celebration of the outpouring of the Holy Spirit.
From 7–15 May, in preparation for the Day of Pentecost, an alternative sequence of daily readings for use at the one of the offices is marked with an asterisk.

			Holy Communion	**Morning Prayer**	**Evening Prayer**
Friday	7 May	W	Acts 18.9–18 Psalm 47.1–6 John 16.20–23	Psalms 20, **81** or **88**, (95) Deuteronomy 29.2–15 1 John 1.1—2.6 *Exodus 35.30—36.1; Galatians 5.13–end	Psalm 145 or **102** Numbers 20.1–13 Luke 7.11–17
Saturday	8 May Julian of Norwich, spiritual writer, c.1417 (see p.84)	W	Acts 18.22–end Psalm 47.1–2, 7–end John 16.23–28	Psalms 21, **47** or 96, **97**, 100 Deuteronomy 30 1 John 2.7–17 *Numbers 11.16–17, 24–29; 1 Corinthians 2	Psalms 84, **85** or **104** Numbers 21.4–9 Luke 7.18–35

Easter 7

Sunday 9 May — 7th Sunday of Easter
Sunday after Ascension Day — W

Principal Service
[Ezekiel 36.24–28]
Acts 1.15–17, 21–end †
Psalm 1
1 John 5.9–13
John 17.6–19

† *The reading from Acts must be used as either the first or second reading.*

3rd Service
Psalm 76
Isaiah 14.3–15
Revelation 14.1–13

2nd Service
Psalm 147.1–12
Isaiah 61
Luke 4.1–21

Monday 10 May — W

Holy Communion
Acts 19.1–8
Psalm 68.1–6
John 16.29–end

Morning Prayer
Psalms 93, 96, 97 or 98, 99, 101
Deuteronomy 31.1–13
1 John 2.18–end
*Numbers 27.15–end; 1 Corinthians 3

Evening Prayer
Psalm 18 or 105* (or 103)
Numbers 22.1–35
Luke 7.36–end

Tuesday 11 May — W

Holy Communion
Acts 20.17–27
Psalm 68.9–10, 18–19
John 17.1–11

Morning Prayer
Psalms 98, 99, 100 or 106* (or 103)
Deuteronomy 31.14–29
1 John 3.1–10
*1 Samuel 10.1–10; 1 Corinthians 12.1–13

Evening Prayer
Psalm 68 or 107*
Numbers 22.36—23.12
Luke 8.1–15

Wednesday 12 May
Gregory Dix, priest, monk, scholar, 1952 — W

Holy Communion
Acts 20.28–end
Psalm 68.27–28, 32–end
John 17.11–19

Morning Prayer
Psalms 2, 29 or 110, 111, 112
Deuteronomy 31.30—32.14
1 John 3.11–end
*1 Kings 19.1–18; Matthew 3.13–end

Evening Prayer
Psalms 36, 46 or 119.129–152
Numbers 23.13–end
Luke 8.16–25

Thursday 13 May — W

Holy Communion
Acts 22.30; 23.6–11
Psalm 16.1, 5–end
John 17.20–end

Morning Prayer
Psalms 24, 72 or 113, 115
Deuteronomy 32.15–47
1 John 4.1–6
*Ezekiel 11.14–20; Matthew 9.35—10.20

Evening Prayer
Psalm 139 or 114, 116, 117
Numbers 24
Luke 8.26–39

or: 1st EP of Matthias the Apostle:
Psalm 147; Isaiah 22.15–22;
Philippians 3.13b—4.1

Friday 14 May
Matthias the Apostle — R

Principal Service
Isaiah 22.15–end or Acts 1.15–end
Psalm 15
Acts 1.15–end or 1 Corinthians 4.1–7
John 15.9–17

3rd Service
MP Psalms 16, 147.1–12
1 Samuel 2.27–35
Acts 2.37–end

2nd Service
EP Psalm 80
1 Samuel 16.1–13a
Matthew 7.15–27

Saturday 15 May — W

Holy Communion
Acts 28.16–20, 30–end
Psalm 11.4–end
John 21.20–end

Morning Prayer
Psalms 42, 43 or 120, 121, 122
Deuteronomy 32.48–end, 34
1 John 5

Evening Prayer
1st EP of Pentecost
Psalm 48
Deuteronomy 16.9–15
John 7.37–39

*Micah 3.1–8; Ephesians 6.10–20 (at MP only)

Pentecost / Ordinary Time

		Principal Service	3rd Service	2nd Service
Sunday	16 May **Pentecost** Whit Sunday	R	Acts 2.1–21 † or Ezekiel 37.1–14 Psalm 104.26–36, 37b [or 104.26–end] Romans 8.22–27 or Acts 2.1–21 † John 15.26–27; 16.4b–15 † The reading from Acts must be used as either the first or second reading.	*MP* Psalm 145 Isaiah 11.1–9 or Wisdom 7.15–23 [24–27] 1 Corinthians 12.4–13	*EP* Psalm 139.1–11 [13–18, 23–24] Ezekiel 36.22–28 Acts 2.22–38 *HC* John 20.19–23
			Holy Communion	**Morning Prayer**	**Evening Prayer**
Monday	17 May DEL week 7 Ordinary Time resumes today.	G	Ecclesiasticus 1.1–10 or James 1.1–11 Psalm 93 or 119.65–72 Mark 9.14–29	Psalms 123, 124, 125, **126** 2 Chronicles 17.1–12 Romans 1.1–17	Psalms **127**, 128, 129 Joshua 1 Luke 9.18–27
Tuesday	18 May	G	Ecclesiasticus 2.1–11 or James 1.12–18 Psalm 37.3–6, 27–28 or 94.12–18 Mark 9.30–37	Psalms **132**, 133 2 Chronicles 18.1–27 Romans 1.18–end	Psalms (134), **135** Joshua 2 Luke 9.28–36
Wednesday	19 May Dunstan, archbishop, monastic reformer, 988 (see p.83)	Gw	Ecclesiasticus 4.11–19 or James 1.19–end Psalm 119.161–168 or 15 Mark 9.38–40	Psalm **119.153–end** 2 Chronicles 18.28—end of 19 Romans 2.1–16	Psalm **136** Joshua 3 Luke 9.37–50
Thursday	20 May Alcuin, deacon, abbot, 804 (see p.84)	Gw	Ecclesiasticus 5.1–8 or James 2.1–9 Psalm 1 or 34.1–7 Mark 9.41–end	Psalms **143**, 146 2 Chronicles 20.1–23 Romans 2.17–end	Psalms **138**, 140, 141 Joshua 4.1—5.1 Luke 9.51–end
Friday	21 May *Helena, protector of the Holy Places, 330*	G	Ecclesiasticus 6.5–17 or James 2.14–24, 26 Psalm 141.19–24 or 112 Mark 10.1–12	Psalms 142, **144** 2 Chronicles 22.10—end of 23 Romans 3.1–20	Psalm **145** Joshua 5.2–end Luke 10.1–16
Saturday	22 May	G	Ecclesiasticus 17.1–15 or James 3.1–10 Psalm 103.13–18 or 12.1–7 Mark 10.13–16	Psalm **147** 2 Chronicles 24.1–22 Romans 3.21–end	1st *EP* of Trinity Sunday Psalms 97, 98 Isaiah 40.12–end Mark 1.1–13

Trinity Sunday

		Principal Service	3rd Service	2nd Service
Sunday 23 May **Trinity Sunday**	Gold or W	Isaiah 6.1–8 Psalm 29 Romans 8.12–17 John 3.1–17	*MP* Psalm 33.1–12 Proverbs 8.1–4, 22–31 2 Corinthians 13.[5–10] 11–end	*EP* Psalm 104.1–10 Ezekiel 1.4–10, 22–28a Revelation 4 *HC* Mark 1.1–13
		Holy Communion	**Morning Prayer**	**Evening Prayer**
Monday 24 May John and Charles Wesley, evangelists, hymn writers, 1791 and 1788 (see p.83) DEL week 8	Gw	Ecclesiasticus 17.24–29 or James 3.13–end Psalm 32.1–8 or 19.7–end Mark 10.17–27	Psalms **1**, 2, 3 2 Chronicles 26.1–21 Romans 4.1–12	Psalms **4**, 7 Joshua 7.1–15 Luke 10.25–37
Tuesday 25 May The Venerable Bede, monk, scholar, historian, 735 (see p.84) Aldhelm, bishop, 709	Gw	Ecclesiasticus 35.1–12 or James 4.1–10 Psalm 50.1–6 or 55.7–9, 24 Mark 10.28–31	Psalms **5**, 6, (8) 2 Chronicles 28 Romans 4.13–end	Psalms **9**, 10* Joshua 7.16–end Luke 10.38–end

Trinity Sunday

If Corpus Christi is kept as a Festival:

		Holy Communion	Morning Prayer	Evening Prayer
Wednesday	**26 May** Gw Augustine, archbishop, 605 (see p.83) John Calvin, reformer, 1564 Philip Neri, founder of the Oratorians, spiritual guide, 1595	Ecclesiasticus 36.1–2, 4–5, 10–17 or James 4.13–17 Psalm 79.8–9, 12, 14 or 49.1–2, 5–10 Mark 10.32–45	Psalm 119.1–32 2 Chronicles 29.1–19 Romans 5.1–11	Psalms 11, 12, 13 Joshua 8.1–29 Luke 11.1–13 or: 1st EP of Corpus Christi: Psalms 110, 111; Exodus 16.2–15; John 6.22–35
		Principal Service	**3rd Service**	**2nd Service**
Thursday	**27 May** W Day of Thanksgiving for the Institution of Holy Communion (Corpus Christi)	Genesis 14.18–20 Psalm 116.10–end 1 Corinthians 11.23–26 John 6.51–58	MP Psalm 147 Deuteronomy 8.2–16 1 Corinthians 10.1–17	EP Psalms 23, 42, 43 Proverbs 9.1–5 Luke 9.11–17

Alternatively, Corpus Christi may be kept as a Lesser Festival, and either these readings or those given for 27 May below may be used.

		Holy Communion	Morning Prayer	Evening Prayer
Friday	**28 May** G Lanfranc, monk, archbishop, scholar, 1089	Ecclesiasticus 44.1, 9–13 or James 5.9–12 Psalm 149.1–5 or 103.1–4, 8–13 Mark 11.11–26	Psalms 17, 19 2 Chronicles 30 Romans 6.1–14	Psalm 22 Joshua 9.3–26 Luke 11.29–36
Saturday	**29 May** G	Ecclesiasticus 51.12b–20a or James 5.13–end Psalm 19.7–end or 141.1–4 Mark 11.27–end	Psalms 20, 21, 23 2 Chronicles 32.1–22 Romans 6.15–end	Psalms 24, 25 Joshua 10.1–15 Luke 11.37–end

If Corpus Christi is not kept as a Festival:

		Holy Communion	Morning Prayer	Evening Prayer
Wednesday	**26 May** Gw Augustine, archbishop, 605 (see p.83) John Calvin, reformer, 1564 Philip Neri, founder of the Oratorians, spiritual guide, 1595	Ecclesiasticus 36.1–2, 4–5, 10–17 or James 4.13–17 Psalm 79.8–9, 12, 14 or 49.1–2, 5–10 Mark 10.32–45	Psalm 119.1–32 2 Chronicles 29.1–19 Romans 5.1–11	Psalms 11, 12, 13 Joshua 8.1–29 Luke 11.1–13
Thursday	**27 May** Gw Day of Thanksgiving for the Institution of Holy Communion (Corpus Christi) *If Corpus Christi is kept as a Lesser Festival, either these readings or those given for 27 May above may be used.*	Ecclesiasticus 42.15–25 or James 5.1–6 Psalm 33.1–9 or 49.1–20 Mark 10.46–end	Psalms 14, 15, 16 2 Chronicles 29.20–end Romans 5.12–end	Psalm 18* Joshua 8.30–end Luke 11.14–28
Friday	**28 May** G Lanfranc, monk, archbishop, scholar, 1089	Ecclesiasticus 44.1, 9–13 or James 5.9–12 Psalm 149.1–5 or 103.1–4, 8–13 Mark 11.11–26	Psalms 17, 19 2 Chronicles 30 Romans 6.1–14	Psalm 22 Joshua 9.3–26 Luke 11.29–36
Saturday	**29 May** G	Ecclesiasticus 51.12b–20a or James 5.13–end Psalm 19.7–end or 141.1–4 Mark 11.27–end	Psalms 20, 21, 23 2 Chronicles 32.1–22 Romans 6.15–end	Psalms 24, 25 Joshua 10.1–15 Luke 11.37–end

Trinity 1

		Principal Service	3rd Service	2nd Service
Sunday	**30 May** G 1st Sunday after Trinity Proper 4	*Continuous:* 1 Samuel 3.1–10 [11–20] Psalm 139.1–5, 12–18 2 Corinthians 4.5–12 Mark 2.23—3.6	Psalms 28, 32 Deuteronomy 5.1–21 Acts 21.17–39a	Psalm 35 [or 35.1–10] Jeremiah 5.1–19 Romans 7.7–end HC Luke 7.1–10
		Related: Deuteronomy 5.12–15 Psalm 81.1–10 2 Corinthians 4.5–12 Mark 2.23—3.6		or: 1st EP of the Visit of the Blessed Virgin Mary to Elizabeth: Psalm 45; Song of Solomon 2.8–14; Luke 1.26–38
Monday	**31 May** W Visit of the Blessed Virgin Mary to Elizabeth	Zephaniah 3.14–18 Psalm 113 Romans 12.9–16 Luke 1.39–49 [50–56]	MP Psalms 85, 150 1 Samuel 2.1–10 Mark 3.31–end	EP Psalms 122, 127, 128 Zechariah 2.10–end John 3.25–30
		Holy Communion	**Morning Prayer**	**Evening Prayer**
Tuesday	**1 June** Gr Justin, martyr, c. 165 (see p.81) DEL week 9	Tobit 2.9–end or 1 Peter 1.10–16 Psalm 112 or 98.1–5 Mark 12.13–17	Psalms 32, **36** 2 Chronicles 34.1–18 Romans 7.7–end	Psalm 33 Joshua 21.43—22.8 Luke 12.13–21
Wednesday	**2 June** G	Tobit 3.1–11, 16–end or 1 Peter 1.18–25 Psalms 25.1–8 or 147.13–end Mark 12.18–27	Psalm **34** 2 Chronicles 34.19–end Romans 8.1–11	Psalm 1**19.33–56** Joshua 22.9–end Luke 12.22–31
Thursday	**3 June** G Martyrs of Uganda, 1885–7, 1977	Tobit 6.10–11, 7.1–15, 8.4–8 or 1 Peter 2.2–5, 9–12 Psalm 128 or 100 Mark 12.28–34	Psalm **37*** 2 Chronicles 35.1–19 Romans 8.12–17	Psalms 39, **40** Joshua 23 Luke 12.32–40
Friday	**4 June** G Petroc, abbot, 6th cent.	Tobit 11.5–15 or 1 Peter 4.7–13 Psalm 146 or 96.10–end Mark 12.35–37	Psalm **31** 2 Chronicles 35.20—36.10 Romans 8.18–30	Psalm 3**5** Joshua 24.1–28 Luke 12.41–48
Saturday	**5 June** Gr Boniface (Wynfrith), bishop, martyr, 754 (see p.81)	Tobit 12.1, 5–15, 20a or Jude 17, 20–25 Psalm 103.1, 8–13 or 63.1–6 Mark 12.38–end	Psalms 41, **42, 43** 2 Chronicles 36.11–end Romans 8.31–end	Psalms 45, **46** Joshua 24.29–end Luke 12.49–end

Trinity 2

		Principal Service		3rd Service	2nd Service
Sunday	**6 June** G 2nd Sunday after Trinity Proper 5	*Continuous:* 1 Samuel 8.4–11 [12–15] 16–20 [11.14–end] Psalm 138	*Related:* Genesis 3.8–15 Psalm 130 2 Corinthians 4.13—5.1 Mark 3.20–end	Psalm 36 Deuteronomy 6.10–end Acts 22.22—23.11	Psalm 37.1–11 [12–17] Jeremiah 6.16–21 Romans 9.1–13 *HC* Luke 7.11–17
		Holy Communion		**Morning Prayer**	**Evening Prayer**
Monday	**7 June** G DEL week 10	2 Corinthians 1.1–7 Psalm 34.1–8 Matthew 5.1–12		Psalm **44** Ezra 1 Romans 9.1–18	Psalms **47**, 49 Judges 2 Luke 13.1–9
Tuesday	**8 June** Gw Thomas Ken, bishop, nonjuror, hymn writer, 1711 (see p.83)	2 Corinthians 1.18–22 Psalm 119.129–136 Matthew 5.13–16		Psalms **48**, 52 Ezra 3 Romans 9.19–end	Psalm **50** Judges 4.1–23 Luke 13.10–21
Wednesday	**9 June** Gw Columba, abbot, missionary, 597 (see p.84) Ephrem, deacon, hymn writer, teacher of the faith, 373	2 Corinthians 3.4–11 Psalm 78.1–4 Matthew 5.17–19		Psalm 119.**57–80** Ezra 4.1–5 Romans 10.1–10	Psalms **59**, 60, (67) Judges 5 Luke 13.22–end
Thursday	**10 June** G	2 Corinthians 3.15—4.1, 3–6 Psalm 78.36–40 Matthew 5.20–26		Psalms 56, **57**, (63*) Ezra 4.7–end Romans 10.11–end	Psalm 61, **62**, 64 Judges 6.1–24 Luke 14.1–11 *or:* 1st EP of Barnabas the Apostle: Psalms 1, 15; Isaiah 42.5–12; Acts 14.8–end
		Principal Service		**3rd Service**	**2nd Service**
Friday	**11 June** R Barnabas the Apostle	Job 29.11–16 or Acts 11.19–end Psalm 112 Acts 11.19–end or Galatians 2.1–10 John 15.12–17		*MP* Psalms 100, 101, 117 Jeremiah 9.23–24 Acts 4.32–end	*EP* Psalm 147 Ecclesiastes 12.9–end or Tobit 4.5–11 Acts 9.26–31
		Holy Communion		**Morning Prayer**	**Evening Prayer**
Saturday	**12 June** G	2 Corinthians 5.14–end Psalm 103.1–12 Matthew 5.33–37		Psalm **68** Ezra 6 Romans 11.13–24	Psalms 65, **66** Judges 7 Luke 14.25–end

Trinity 3

		Principal Service		3rd Service	2nd Service
Sunday	13 June G 3rd Sunday after Trinity Proper 6	Continuous: 1 Samuel 15.34—16.13 Psalm 20	Related: Ezekiel 17.22–end Psalm 92.1-4, 12–end [or 92.1–8] 2 Corinthians 5.6–10 [11–13] 14–17 Mark 4.26-34	Psalms 42, 43 Deuteronomy 10.12—11.1 Acts 23.12-35	Psalm 39 Jeremiah 7.1–16 Romans 9.14-26 HC Luke 7.36—8.3

		Holy Communion	Morning Prayer	Evening Prayer
Monday	14 June G Richard Baxter, puritan divine, 1691 DEL week 11	2 Corinthians 6.1–10 Psalm 98 Matthew 5.38-42	Psalm 71 Ezra 7 Romans 11.25–end	Psalms 72, 75 Judges 8.22–end Luke 15.1–10
Tuesday	15 June G Evelyn Underhill, spiritual writer, 1941	2 Corinthians 8.1–9 Psalm 146 Matthew 5.43–end	Psalm 73 Ezra 8.15–end Romans 12.1–8	Psalm 74 Judges 9.1–21 Luke 15.11–end
Wednesday	16 June Gw Richard, bishop, 1253 (see p.83) Joseph Butler, bishop, philosopher, 1752	2 Corinthians 9.6–11 Psalm 112 Matthew 6.1–6, 16-18	Psalm 77 Ezra 9 Romans 12.9–end	Psalm 119.81–104 Judges 9.22–end Luke 16.1–18
Thursday	17 June G Samuel and Henrietta Barnett, social reformers, 1913 and 1936	2 Corinthians 11.1–11 Psalm 111 Matthew 6.7–15	Psalm 78.1–39* Ezra 10.1–17 Romans 13.1–7	Psalm 78.40–end* Judges 11.1–11 Luke 16.19–end
Friday	18 June G Bernard Mizeki, martyr, 1896	2 Corinthians 11.18, 21b-30 Psalm 34.1–6 Matthew 6.19–23	Psalm 55 Nehemiah 1 Romans 13.8–end	Psalm 69 Judges 11.29–end Luke 17.1–10
Saturday	19 June G Sundar Singh, sadhu (holy man), evangelist, teacher of the faith, 1929	2 Corinthians 12.1–10 Psalm 89.20-33 Matthew 6.24–end	Psalms 76, 79 Nehemiah 2 Romans 14.1–12	Psalms 81, 84 Judges 12.1–7 Luke 17.11–19

Trinity 4

Sunday 20 June — 4th Sunday after Trinity — G
Proper 7

Principal Service
Continuous:
1 Samuel 17.[1a, 4–11, 19–23] 32–49
Psalm 9.9–end
or 1 Samuel 17.57—18.5, 10–16
Psalm 133

Related: Job 38.1–11
Psalm 107.1–3, 23–end [or 107.23–end]

2 Corinthians 6.1–13
Mark 4.35–end

3rd Service
Psalm 48
Deuteronomy 11.1–15
Acts 27.1–12

2nd Service
Psalm 49
Jeremiah 10.1–16
Romans 11.25–end
HC Luke 8.26–39

Monday 21 June — G
DEL week 12

Holy Communion
Genesis 12.1–9
Psalm 33.12–end
Matthew 7.1–5

Morning Prayer
Psalms 80, 82
Nehemiah 4
Romans 14.13–end

Evening Prayer
Psalms 85, 86
Judges 13.1–24
Luke 17.20–end

Tuesday 22 June — Gr
Alban, first martyr of Britain, c.250 (see p.81)

Genesis 13.2, 5–end
Psalm 15
Matthew 7.6, 12–14

Psalms 87, **89**.1–18
Nehemiah 5
Romans 15.1–13

Psalm **89**.19–end
Judges 14
Luke 18.1–14

Wednesday 23 June — Gw
Etheldreda, abbess, c.678 (see p.84)
Ember Day

Genesis 15.1–12, 17–18
Psalm 105.1–9
Matthew 7.15–20

Psalm 119.**105–128**
Nehemiah 6.1—7.4
Romans 15.14–21

Psalms **91**, 93
Judges 15.1—16.3
Luke 18.15–30
or: 1st EP of the Birth of John the Baptist:
Psalm 71; Judges 13.2–7, 24–end;
Luke 1.5–25

Thursday 24 June — W
Birth of John the Baptist

Principal Service
Isaiah 40.1–11
Psalm 85.7–end
Acts 13.14b–26 or Galatians 3.23–end
Luke 1.57–66, 80

3rd Service
MP Psalms 50, 149
Ecclesiasticus 48.1–10
or Malachi 3.1–6
Luke 3.1–17

2nd Service
EP Psalms 80, 82
Malachi 4
Matthew 11.2–19

Friday 25 June — G
Ember Day

Holy Communion
Genesis 17.1, 9–10, 15–22
Psalm 128
Matthew 8.1–4

Morning Prayer
Psalms **88**, (95)
Nehemiah 9.1–23
Romans 16.1–16

Evening Prayer
Psalm 102
Judges 17
Luke 19.1–10

Saturday 26 June — G
Ember Day

Genesis 18.1–15
Canticle: Luke 1.46b–55
Matthew 8.5–17

Psalms 96, **97**, 100
Nehemiah 9.24–end
Romans 16.17–end

Psalm 104
Judges 18
Luke 19.11–27

Trinity 5

Sunday 27 June
5th Sunday after Trinity G
Proper 8

Principal Service
Continuous:
2 Samuel 1.1,17–end
Psalm 130

Related:
Wisdom 1.13–15; 2.23–24 †
Canticle:
Lamentations 3.23–33
or Psalm 30
† Lamentations 3.23–33
may be read as the first reading
in place of Wisdom 1.13–15; 2.23–24
2 Corinthians 8.7–end
Mark 5.21–end

3rd Service
Psalm 56
Deuteronomy 15.1–11
Acts 27.[13–32] 33–end

2nd Service
Psalms [52] 53
Jeremiah 11.1–14
Romans 13.1–10
HC Luke 9.51–end

Monday 28 June
Irenaeus, bishop, teacher of the faith, Gw
c.200 (see p.82)
DEL week 13

Holy Communion
Genesis 18.16–end
Psalm 103.6–17
Matthew 8.18–22

Morning Prayer
Psalms **98**, 99, 101
Nehemiah 12.27–47
2 Corinthians 1.1–14
or: 1st EP of Peter and Paul, Apostles [or †Peter the Apostle alone]:

Evening Prayer
Psalm **105*** (or 103)
1 Samuel 1.1–20
Luke 19.28–40
Psalms 66, 67; Ezekiel 3.4–11;
Galatians 1.13—2.8 [†Acts 9.32–end]

Tuesday 29 June
Peter and Paul, Apostles R
or
Peter the Apostle R

Principal Service
Peter and Paul:
Zechariah 4.1–6a, 10b–end
or Acts 12.1–11
Psalm 125
Acts 12.1–11
or 2 Timothy 4.6–8, 17–18
Matthew 16.13–19

Peter alone:
Ezekiel 3.22–end
or Acts 12.1–11
Psalm 125
Acts 12.1–11
or 1 Peter 2.19–end
Matthew 16.13–19

3rd Service
MP Psalms 71, 113
Isaiah 49.1–6
Acts 11.1–18

2nd Service
EP Psalms 124, 138
Ezekiel 34.11–16
John 21.15–22

Trinity 5

		Holy Communion	Morning Prayer	Evening Prayer
Wednesday	30 June G	Genesis 21.5, 8–20 Psalm 34.1–12 Matthew 8.28–end	Psalms 110, **111**, 112 Nehemiah 13.15–end 2 Corinthians 2.5–end	Psalm 119.**129–152** 1 Samuel 2.12–26 Luke 20.1–8
Thursday	1 July G *Henry, John, and Henry Venn, priests,* *evangelical divines, 1797, 1813, 1873*	Genesis 22.1–19 Psalm 116.1–7 Matthew 9.1–8	Psalms 113, **115** Esther 1 2 Corinthians 3	Psalms 114, **116**, 117 1 Samuel 2.27–end Luke 20.9–19
Friday	2 July G	Genesis 23.1–4, 19, 24.1–8, 62–end Psalm 106.1–5 Matthew 9.9–13	Psalm **139** Esther 2 2 Corinthians 4	Psalms **130**, 131, 137 1 Samuel 3.1—4.1a Luke 20.20–26 *or:* 1st EP of Thomas the Apostle: Psalm 27: Isaiah 35; Hebrews 10.35—11.1

		Principal Service	3rd Service	2nd Service
Saturday	3 July R Thomas the Apostle	Habakkuk 2.1–4 Psalm 31.1–6 Ephesians 2.19–end John 20.24–29	*MP* Psalms 92, 146 2 Samuel 15.17–21 *or* Ecclesiasticus 2 John 11.1–16	*EP* Psalm 139 Job 42.1–6 1 Peter 1.3–12

Trinity 6

		Principal Service		3rd Service	2nd Service
Sunday	**4 July** **6th Sunday after Trinity** Proper 9 — G	*Continuous:* 2 Samuel 5.1–5, 9–10 Psalm 48	*Related:* Ezekiel 2.1–5 Psalm 123 2 Corinthians 12.2–10 Mark 6.1–13	Psalm 57 Deuteronomy 24.10–end Acts 28.1–16	Psalms [63] 64 Jeremiah 20.1–11*a* Romans 14.1–17 HC Luke 10.1–11, 16–20
		Holy Communion		**Morning Prayer**	**Evening Prayer**
Monday	**5 July** DEL week 14 — G	Genesis 28.10–end Psalm 91.1–10 Matthew 9.18–26		Psalms 123, 124, 125, **126** Esther 4 2 Corinthians 6.1—7.1	Psalms **127**, 128, 129 1 Samuel 5 Luke 20.41—21.4
Tuesday	**6 July** Thomas More, scholar, and John Fisher, bishop, martyrs, 1535 — G	Genesis 32.22–end Psalm 17.1–8 Matthew 9.32–end		Psalms **132**, 133 Esther 5 2 Corinthians 7.2–end	Psalms (134), **135** 1 Samuel 6.1–16 Luke 21.5–19
Wednesday	**7 July** — G	Genesis 41.55–end, 42.5–7, 17–end Psalm 33.1–4, 18–end Matthew 10.1–7		Psalm **119.153–end** Esther 6.1–13 2 Corinthians 8.1–15	Psalm **136** 1 Samuel 7 Luke 21.20–28
Thursday	**8 July** — G	Genesis 44.18–21, 23–29, 45.1–5 Psalm 105.11–17 Matthew 10.7–15		Psalms **138**, 140, 141 Esther 6.14—end of 7 2 Corinthians 8.16—9.5	Psalms **138**, 140, 141 1 Samuel 8 Luke 21.29–end
Friday	**9 July** — G	Genesis 46.1–7, 28–30 Psalm 37.3–6, 27–28 Matthew 10.16–23		Psalms 142, **144** Esther 8 2 Corinthians 9.6–end	Psalm **145** 1 Samuel 9.1–14 Luke 22.1–13
Saturday	**10 July** — G	Genesis 49.29–end, 50.15–25 Psalm 105.1–7 Matthew 10.24–33		Psalm **147** Esther 9.20–28 2 Corinthians 10	Psalms **148**, 149, 150 1 Samuel 9.15—10.1 Luke 22.14–23

Trinity 7

Sunday — 11 July
7th Sunday after Trinity — G
Proper 10

Principal Service
Continuous:
2 Samuel 6.1–5, 12b–19
Psalm 24

Related:
Amos 7.7–15
Psalm 85.8–end
Ephesians 1.3–14
Mark 6.14–29

3rd Service
Psalm 65
Deuteronomy 28.1–14
Acts 28.17–end

2nd Service
Psalm 66 [or 66.1–8]
Job 4.1; 5.6–end
or Ecclesiasticus 4.11–end
Romans 15.14–29
HC Luke 10.25–37

Holy Communion / Morning Prayer / Evening Prayer

Monday — 12 July — G
DEL week 15

Principal Service
Exodus 1.8–14, 22
Psalm 124
Matthew 10.34—11.1

3rd Service
Psalms 1, 2, 3
Jeremiah 26
2 Corinthians 11.1–15

2nd Service
Psalms **4**, 7
1 Samuel 10.1–16
Luke 22.24–30

Tuesday — 13 July — G

Exodus 2.1–15
Psalm 69.1–2, 31–end
Matthew 11.20–24

Psalms **5**, 6, (8)
Jeremiah 28
2 Corinthians 11.16–end

Psalms **9**, 10
1 Samuel 10.17–end
Luke 22.31–38

Wednesday — 14 July — Gw
John Keble, priest, poet, 1866 (see p.83)

Exodus 3.1–6, 9–12
Psalm 103.1–7
Matthew 11.25–27

Psalm **119.1–32**
Jeremiah 29.1–14
2 Corinthians 12

Psalms **11**, 12, 13
1 Samuel 11
Luke 22.39–46

Thursday — 15 July — Gw
Swithun, bishop, c.862 (see p.83)
*Bonaventure, friar, bishop,
teacher of the faith, 1274*

Exodus 3.13–20
Psalm 105.1–2, 23
Matthew 11.28–end

Psalms 14, **15**, 16
Jeremiah 30.1–11
2 Corinthians 13

Psalm **18***
1 Samuel 12
Luke 22.47–62

Friday — 16 July — G
Osmund, bishop, 1099

Exodus 11.10—12.14
Psalm 116.10–end
Matthew 12.1–8

Psalms 17, **19**
Jeremiah 30.12–22
James 1.1–11

Psalm **22**
1 Samuel 13.5–18
Luke 22.63–end

Saturday — 17 July — G

Exodus 12.37–42
Psalm 136.1–4, 10–15
Matthew 12.14–21

Psalms 20, 21, **23**
Jeremiah 31.1–22
James 1.12–end

Psalms **24**, 25
1 Samuel 13.19—14.15
Luke 23.1–12

Trinity 8

Sunday 18 July
8th Sunday after Trinity
Proper 11
G

Principal Service
Continuous:
2 Samuel 7.1—14a
Psalm 89.20–37

Related:
Jeremiah 23.1–6
Psalm 23
Ephesians 2.11–end
Mark 6.30–34, 53–end

3rd Service
Psalms 67, 70
Deuteronomy 30.1–10
1 Peter 3.8–18

2nd Service
Psalm 73 [or 73.21–end]
Job 13.13—14.6
or Ecclesiasticus 18.1–14
Hebrews 2.5–end
HC Luke 10.38–end

Holy Communion
Morning Prayer
Evening Prayer

Monday 19 July
Gregory, bishop, and his sister Macrina, deaconess, teachers of the faith, c.394 and c.379 (see p.82)
DEL week 16
Gw

Exodus 14.5–18
Psalm 136.1–4, 10–15 or *Canticle:* Exodus 15.1–6
Matthew 12.38–42

Psalms 27, **30**
Jeremiah 31.23–25, 27–37
James 2.1–13

Psalms 26, **28, 29**
1 Samuel 14.24–46
Luke 23.13–25

Tuesday 20 July
Margaret of Antioch, martyr, 4th cent.
Bartolomé de las Casas, Apostle to the Indies, 1566
G

Exodus 14.21—15.1
Psalm 105.37–44 or *Canticle:* Exodus 15.8–10, 12, 17
Matthew 12.46–end

Psalms 32, **36**
Jeremiah 32.1–15
James 2.14–end

Psalm **33**
1 Samuel 15.1–23
Luke 23.26–43

Wednesday 21 July
G

Exodus 16.1–5, 9–15
Psalm 78.17–31
Matthew 13.1–9

Psalm **34**
Jeremiah 33.1–13
James 3

Psalm 119.33–56
1 Samuel 16
Luke 23.44–56a
or: 1st EP of Mary Magdalene:
Psalm 139; Isaiah 25.1–9;
2 Corinthians 1.3–7

Thursday 22 July
Mary Magdalene
W

Principal Service
Song of Solomon 3.1–4
Psalm 42.1–10
2 Corinthians 5.14–17
John 20.1–2, 11–18

3rd Service
MP Psalms 30, 32, 150
1 Samuel 16.14–end
Luke 8.1–3

2nd Service
EP Psalm 63
Zephaniah 3.14–end
Mark 15.40—16.7

Holy Communion
Morning Prayer
Evening Prayer

Friday 23 July
Bridget, abbess, 1373
G

Exodus 20.1–17
Psalm 19.7–11
Matthew 13.18–23

Psalm 3 1
Jeremiah 35
James 4.13—5.6

Psalm **35**
1 Samuel 17.31–54
Luke 24.13–35

Saturday 24 July
G

Exodus 24.3–8
Psalm 50.1–6, 14–15
Matthew 13.24–30

Psalms 41, **42, 43**
Jeremiah 36.1–18
James 5.7–end

Psalms 45, **46**
1 Samuel 17.55—18.16
Luke 24.36–end
Or, if James the Apostle is celebrated on 25 July 1st EP of James the Apostle:
Psalm 144; Deuteronomy 30.11—end;
Mark 5.21—end

James / Trinity 9

If James the Apostle is celebrated on Sunday 25 July:

Sunday 25 July — James the Apostle (R)

Principal Service
Jeremiah 45.1–5 or Acts 11.27—12.2
Psalm 126
Acts 11.27—12.2 or 2 Corinthians 4.7–15
Matthew 20.20–28

3rd Service
MP Psalms 7, 29, 117
2 Kings 1.9–15
Luke 9.46–56

2nd Service
EP Psalm 94
Jeremiah 26.1–15
Mark 1.14–20

Monday 26 July — Anne and Joachim, parents of the Blessed Virgin Mary (Gw)
DEL week 17

Holy Communion
Exodus 32.15–24, 30–34
Psalm 106.19–23
Matthew 13.31–35
Lesser Festival eucharistic lectionary:
Zephaniah 3.14–18a
Psalm 127
Romans 8.28–30
Matthew 13.16–17

Morning Prayer
Psalm 44
Jeremiah 36.19–end
Mark 1.1–13

Evening Prayer
Psalms 47, 49
1 Samuel 19.1–18
Acts 1.1–14

If James the Apostle is transferred to Monday 26 July:

Sunday 25 July — 9th Sunday after Trinity (G)
Proper 12

Principal Service
Continuous:
2 Samuel 11.1–15
Psalm 14

Related:
2 Kings 4.42–end
Psalm 145.10–19
Ephesians 3.14–end
John 6.1–21

3rd Service
Psalm 75
Song of Solomon 2
or 1 Maccabees 2.[1–14] 15–22
1 Peter 4.7–14

2nd Service
Psalm 74 [or 74.11–16]
Job 19.1–27a
or Ecclesiasticus 38.24–end
Hebrews 8
HC Luke 11.1–13
or: 1st EP of James the Apostle:
Psalm 144; Deuteronomy 30.11–end;
Mark 5.21–end

Monday 26 July — James the Apostle (R)
Transferred from 25 July

Principal Service
Jeremiah 45.1–5 or Acts 11.27—12.2
Psalm 126
Acts 11.27—12.2 or 2 Corinthians 4.7–15
Matthew 20.20–28

3rd Service
MP Psalms 7, 29, 117
2 Kings 1.9–15
Luke 9.46–56

2nd Service
EP Psalm 94
Jeremiah 26.1–15
Mark 1.14–20

Trinity 9

		Holy Communion	Morning Prayer	Evening Prayer
Tuesday	**27 July** G *Brooke Foss Westcott, bishop,* *teacher of the faith, 1901* DEL week 17	Exodus 33.7–11, 34.5–9, 28 Psalm 103.8–12 Matthew 13.36–43	Psalms **48**, 52 Jeremiah 37 Mark 1.14–20	Psalm **50** 1 Samuel 20.1–17 Acts 1.15–end
Wednesday	**28 July** G	Exodus 34.29–end Psalm 99 Matthew 13.44–46	Psalm 119.**57–80** Jeremiah 38.1–13 Mark 1.21–28	Psalms **59**, 60 (67) 1 Samuel 20.18–end Acts 2.1–21
Thursday	**29 July** Gw *Mary, Martha and Lazarus,* *companions of Our Lord*	Exodus 40.16–21, 34–end Psalm 84.1–6 Matthew 13. 47–53 *Lesser Festival eucharistic lectionary:* Isaiah 25.6–9 Psalm 49.5–10, 16 Hebrews 2.10–15 John 12.1–8	Psalms 56, **57** (63*) Jeremiah 38.14–end Mark 1.29–end	Psalms 61, **62**, 64 1 Samuel 21.1—22.5 Acts 2.22–36
Friday	**30 July** Gw *William Wilberforce, social reformer,* *Olaudah Equiano and Thomas Clarkson* *anti-slavery campaigners,* *1833, 1797 and 1846 (see p.85)*	Leviticus 23.1, 4–11, 15–16, 27, 34–37 Psalm 81.1–8 Matthew 13.54–end	Psalms **51**, 54 Jeremiah 39 Mark 2.1–12	Psalm **38** 1 Samuel 22.6–end Acts 2.37–end
Saturday	**31 July** G *Ignatius of Loyola, founder of the* *Society of Jesus, 1556*	Leviticus 25.1, 8–17 Psalm 67 Matthew 14.1–12	Psalm **68** Jeremiah 40 Mark 2.13–22	Psalms 65, **66** 1 Samuel 23 Acts 3.1–10

Trinity 10

Sunday 1 August — 10th Sunday after Trinity — G
Proper 13

Principal Service

Continuous:
2 Samuel 11.26—12.13a
Psalm 51.1–13

Related:
Exodus 16.2–4, 9–15
Psalm 78.23–29
Ephesians 4.1–16
John 6.24–35

3rd Service
Psalm 86
Song of Solomon 5.2–end
or 1 Maccabees 3.1–12
2 Peter 1.1–15

2nd Service
Psalm 88 [or 88.1–10]
Job 28
or Ecclesiasticus 42.15–end
Hebrews 11.17–31
HC Luke 12.13–21

Monday 2 August — DEL week 18 — G

Holy Communion
Numbers 11.4–15
Psalm 81.11–end
Matthew 14.13–21 or 14.22–end

Morning Prayer
Psalm 71
Jeremiah 41
Mark 2.23—3.6

Evening Prayer
Psalms 72, 75
1 Samuel 24
Acts 3.11–end

Tuesday 3 August — G

Numbers 12.1–13
Psalm 51.1–8
Matthew 14.22–end or 15.1–2, 10–14

Psalm 73
Jeremiah 42
Mark 3.7–19a

Psalm 74
1 Samuel 26
Acts 4.1–12

Wednesday 4 August — G
Jean-Baptiste Vianney, curé d'Ars, spiritual guide, 1859

Numbers 13.1–2, 25—14.1, 26–35
Psalm 106.14–24
Matthew 15.21–28

Psalm 77
Jeremiah 43
Mark 3.19b–end

Psalm 119.81–104
1 Samuel 28.3–end
Acts 4.13–31

Thursday 5 August — Gr
Oswald, king, martyr, 642 (see p.81)

Numbers 20.1–13
Psalm 95.1, 8–end
Matthew 16.13–23

Psalm 78.1–39*
Jeremiah 44.1–14
Mark 4.1–20

Psalm 78.40–end*
1 Samuel 31
Acts 4.32—5.11
or: 1st EP of the Transfiguration of Our Lord:
Psalms 99, 110; Exodus 24.12–end;
John 12.27–36a

Friday 6 August — Transfiguration of Our Lord — Gold or W

Principal Service
Daniel 7.9–10, 13–14
Psalm 97
2 Peter 1.16–19
Luke 9.28–36

Holy Communion

3rd Service
MP Psalms 27, 150
Ecclesiasticus 48.1–10
or 1 Kings 19.1–16
1 John 3.1–3

2nd Service
EP Psalm 72
Exodus 34.29–end
2 Corinthians 3

Saturday 7 August — G
John Mason Neale, priest, hymn writer, 1866

Deuteronomy 6.4–13
Psalm 18.1–2, 48–end
Matthew 17.14–20

Morning Prayer
Psalms 76, 79
Jeremiah 45
Mark 4.35–end

Evening Prayer
Psalms 81, 84
2 Samuel 2.1–11
Acts 5.27–end

Trinity 11

		Principal Service	3rd Service	2nd Service
Sunday	**8 August** G 11th Sunday after Trinity Proper 14	*Continuous:* 2 Samuel 18.5–9, 15, 31–33 Psalm 130 *Related:* 1 Kings 19.4–8 Psalm 34.1–8 Ephesians 4.25 — 5.2 John 6.35, 41–51	Psalm 90 Song of Solomon 8.5–7 or 1 Maccabees 14.4–15 2 Peter 3.8–13	Psalm 91 [or 91.1–12] Job 39.1 — 40.4 or Ecclesiasticus 43.13–end Hebrews 12.1–17 HC Luke 12.32–40
		Holy Communion	**Morning Prayer**	**Evening Prayer**
Monday	**9 August** Gw Mary Sumner, founder of the Mothers' Union, 1921 (see p.85) DEL week 19	Deuteronomy 10.12–end Psalm 147.13–end Matthew 17.22–end	Psalms 80, 82 Micah 1.1–9 Mark 5.1–20	Psalms 85, 86 2 Samuel 3.12–end Acts 6
Tuesday	**10 August** Gr Laurence, deacon, martyr, 258 (see p.81)	Deuteronomy 31.1–8 Psalm 107.1–3, 42–end or *Canticle:* Deuteronomy 32.3–4, 7–9 Matthew 18.1–5, 10, 12–14	Psalm 87, **89.1–18** Micah 2 Mark 5.21–34	Psalm **89.19–end** 2 Samuel 5.1–12 Acts 7.1–16
Wednesday	**11 August** Gw Clare of Assisi, founder of the Poor Clares, 1253 (see p.84) *John Henry Newman, priest, 1890*	Deuteronomy 34 Psalm 66.14–end Matthew 18.15–20	Psalm **119.105–128** Micah 3 Mark 5.35–end	Psalm **91**, 93 2 Samuel 6.1–19 Acts 7.17–43
Thursday	**12 August** G	Joshua 3.7–11, 13–17 Psalm 114 Matthew 18.21 — 19.1	Psalms 90, **92** Micah 4.1 — 5.1 Mark 6.1–13	Psalm **94** 2 Samuel 7.1–17 Acts 7.44–53
Friday	**13 August** Gw Jeremy Taylor, bishop, teacher of the faith, 1667 (see p.82) *Florence Nightingale, nurse,* *social reformer, 1910* *Octavia Hill, social reformer, 1912*	Joshua 24.1–13 Psalm 136.1–3, 16–22 Matthew 19.3–12	Psalms **88**, (95) Micah 5.2–end Mark 6.14–29	Psalm **102** 2 Samuel 7.18–end Acts 7.54 — 8.3
Saturday	**14 August** G *Maximilian Kolbe, friar, martyr, 1941*	Joshua 24.14–29 Psalm 16.1, 5–end Matthew 19.13–15	Psalms 96, **97**, 100 Micah 6 Mark 6.30–44	Psalm **104** 2 Samuel 9 Acts 8.4–25 Or, if The Blessed Virgin Mary is celebrated on 15 August: 1st EP of the Blessed Virgin Mary: Psalm 72; Proverbs 8.22–31; John 19.23–27

The Blessed Virgin Mary is celebrated on 15 August

The Blessed Virgin Mary / Trinity 12

If The Blessed Virgin Mary is celebrated on Sunday 15 August:

		Principal Service	**3rd Service**	**2nd Service**
Sunday	**15 August** W The Blessed Virgin Mary	Isaiah 61.10–end or Revelation 11.19—12.6, 10 Psalm 45.10–end Galatians 4.4–7 Luke 1.46–55	MP Psalms 98, 138, 147.1–12 Isaiah 7.10–15 Luke 11.27–28	EP Psalm 132 Song of Solomon 2.1–7 Acts 1.6–14
		Holy Communion	**Morning Prayer**	**Evening Prayer**
Monday	**16 August** G DEL week 20	Judges 2.11–19 Psalm 106.34–42 Matthew 19.16–22	Psalms 98, 99, 101 Micah 7.1–7 Mark 6.45–end	Psalm 105* (or 103) 2 Samuel 11 Acts 8.26–end

If The Blessed Virgin Mary is transferred to Monday 16 August:

		Principal Service	**3rd Service**	**2nd Service**
Sunday	**15 August** G 12th Sunday after Trinity Proper 15	*Continuous:* 1 Kings 2.10–12; 3.3–14 Psalm 111 *Related:* Proverbs 9.1–6 Psalm 34.9–14 Ephesians 5.15–20 John 6.51–58	Psalms [92] 100 Exodus 2.23—3.10 Hebrews 13.1–15 HC Luke 12.49–56	Psalm 106.1–10 Jonah 1 or Ecclesiasticus 3.1–15 2 Peter 3.14–end *or:* 1st EP of the Blessed Virgin Mary: Psalm 72; Proverbs 8.22–31; John 19.23–27
Monday	**16 August** W The Blessed Virgin Mary *Transferred from 15 August*	Isaiah 61.10–end or Revelation 11.19—12.6, 10 Psalm 45.10–end Galatians 4.4–7 Luke 1.46–55	MP Psalms 98, 138, 147.1–12 Isaiah 7.10–15 Luke 11.27–28	EP Psalm 132 Song of Solomon 2.1–7 Acts 1.6–14

Trinity 12

		Holy Communion	Morning Prayer	Evening Prayer
Tuesday **17 August** DEL week 20	G	Judges 6.11–24 Psalm 85.8–end Matthew 19.23–end	Psalm **106*** (or 103) Micah 7.8–end Mark 7.1–13	Psalm **107*** 2 Samuel 12.1–25 Acts 9.1–19a
Wednesday 18 August	G	Judges 9.6–15 Psalm 21.1–6 Matthew 20.1–16	Psalms 110, **111**, 112 Habakkuk 1.1–11 Mark 7.14–23	Psalm **119.129–152** 2 Samuel 15.1–12 Acts 9.19b–31
Thursday 19 August	G	Judges 11.29–end Psalm 40.4–11 Matthew 22.1–14	Psalms 113, **115** Habakkuk 1.12—2.5 Mark 7.24–30	Psalms 114, **116**, 117 2 Samuel 15.13–end Acts 9.32–end
Friday 20 August Bernard, abbot, teacher of the faith, 1153 (see p.82) William and Catherine Booth, founders of the Salvation Army, 1912, 1890	Gw	Ruth 1.1, 3–6, 14–16, 22 Psalm 146 Matthew 22.34–40	Psalm **139** Habakkuk 2.6–end Mark 7.31–end	Psalms **130**, 131, 137 2 Samuel 16.1–14 Acts 10.1–16
Saturday 21 August	G	Ruth 2.1–3, 8–11, 4.13–17 Psalm 128 Matthew 23.1–12	Psalms 120, **121**, 122 Habakkuk 3.2–19a Mark 8.1–10	Psalm **118** 2 Samuel 17.1–23 Acts 10.17–33

Trinity 13

		Principal Service	3rd Service	2nd Service
Sunday	**22 August** G 13th Sunday after Trinity Proper 16	*Continuous:* 1 Kings 8.[1, 6, 10–11] 22–30, 41–43 Psalm 84 *Related:* Joshua 24.1–2a, 14–18 Psalm 34.15–end Ephesians 6.10–20 John 6.56–69	Psalm 115 Jonah 2 *or* Ecclesiasticus 3.17–29 Revelation 1	Psalm 116 [*or* 116.10–end] Exodus 4.27—5.1 Hebrews 13.16–21 HC Luke 13.10–17
		Holy Communion	**Morning Prayer**	**Evening Prayer**
Monday	**23 August** G DEL week 21	1 Thessalonians 1.1–5, 8–end Psalm 149.1–5 Matthew 23.13–22	Psalms 123, 124, 125, **126** Haggai 1.1–11 Mark 8.11–21	Psalms **127**, 128, 129 2 Samuel 18.1–18 Acts 10.34–end *or:* 1st EP of Bartholomew the Apostle: Psalm 97; Isaiah 61.1–9; 2 Corinthians 6.1–10
		Principal Service	**3rd Service**	**2nd Service**
Tuesday	**24 August** R Bartholomew the Apostle	Isaiah 43.8–13 *or* Acts 5.12–16 Psalm 145.1–7 Acts 5.12–16 *or* 1 Corinthians 4.9–15 Luke 22.24–30	MP Psalms 86, 117 Genesis 28.10–17 John 1.43–end	EP Psalms 91, 116 Ecclesiasticus 39.1–10 *or* Deuteronomy 18.15–19 Matthew 10.1–22
		Holy Communion	**Morning Prayer**	**Evening Prayer**
Wednesday	**25 August** G	1 Thessalonians 2.9–13 Psalm 126 Matthew 23.27–32	Psalm 119.**153–end** Haggai 2.10–end Mark 8.27—9.1	Psalm **136** 2 Samuel 19.8b–23 Acts 11.19–end
Thursday	**26 August** G	1 Thessalonians 3.7–end Psalm 90.13–end Matthew 24.42–end	Psalms **143**, 146 Zechariah 1.1–17 Mark 9.2–13	Psalms **138**, 140, 141 2 Samuel 19.24–end Acts 12.1–17
Friday	**27 August** Gw Monica, mother of Augustine of Hippo, 387 (see p.85)	1 Thessalonians 4.1–8 Psalm 97 Matthew 25.1–13	Psalms 142, **144** Zechariah 1.18—end of 2 Mark 9.14–29	Psalm **145** 2 Samuel 23.1–7 Acts 12.18–end
Saturday	**28 August** Gw Augustine, bishop, teacher of the faith, 430 (see p.82)	1 Thessalonians 4.9–12 Psalm 98.1–2, 8–end Matthew 25.14–30	Psalm **147** Zechariah 3 Mark 9.30–37	Psalms **148**, 149, 150 2 Samuel 24 Acts 13.1–12

Trinity 14

		Principal Service		3rd Service	2nd Service
Sunday	**29 August** G **14th Sunday after Trinity** Proper 17	Continuous: Song of Solomon 2.8–13 Psalm 45.1–2, 6–9 [or 45.1–7]	Related: Deuteronomy 4.1–2, 6–9 Psalm 15	Psalm 119.17–40 Jonah 3.1–9 or Ecclesiasticus 11.7–28 (or 19–28) Revelation 3.14–end	Psalm 119.1–16 [or 119.9–16] Exodus 12.21–27 Matthew 4.23—5.20
		James 1.17–end Mark 7.1–8, 14, 15, 21–23			
		Holy Communion		**Morning Prayer**	**Evening Prayer**
Monday	**30 August** Gw John Bunyan, spiritual writer, 1688 (see p.82) DEL week 22	1 Thessalonians 4.13–end Psalm 96 Luke 4.16–30		Psalms **1**, 2, 3 Zechariah 4 Mark 9.38–end	Psalms **4**, 7 1 Kings 1.5–31 Acts 13.13–43
Tuesday	**31 August** Gw Aidan, bishop, missionary, 651 (see p.84)	1 Thessalonians 5.1–6, 9–11 Psalm 27.1–8 Luke 4.31–37		Psalms **5**, 6 (8) Zechariah 6.9–end Mark 10.1–16	Psalms **9**, 10* 1 Kings 1.32—2.4; 2.10–12 Acts 13.44—14.7
Wednesday	**1 September** G *Giles, hermit, c.710*	Colossians 1.1–8 Psalm 34.11–18 Luke 4.38–end		Psalm 119.**1–32** Zechariah 7 Mark 10.17–31	Psalms **11**, 12, 13 1 Kings 3 Acts 14.8–end
Thursday	**2 September** G *Martyrs of Papua New Guinea, 1901, 1942*	Colossians 1.9–14 Psalm 98.1–5 Luke 5.1–11		Psalms 14, **15**, 16 Zechariah 8.1–8 Mark 10.32–34	Psalm **18*** 1 Kings 4.29—5.12 Acts 15.1–21
Friday	**3 September** Gw Gregory the Great, bishop, teacher of the faith, 604 (see p.82)	Colossians 1.15–20 Psalm 89.19b–28 Luke 5.33–end		Psalms 17, **19** Zechariah 8.9–end Mark 10.35–45	Psalm **22** 1 Kings 6.1, 11–28 Acts 15.22–35
Saturday	**4 September** G *Birinus, bishop, 650*	Colossians 1.21–23 Psalm 117 Luke 6.1–5		Psalms 20, 21, **23** Zechariah 9.1–12 Mark 10.46–end	Psalms **24**, 25 1 Kings 8.1–30 Acts 15.36—16.5

Trinity 15

Sunday

5 September
15th Sunday after Trinity — G
Proper 18

Principal Service
Continuous:
Proverbs 22.1–2, 8, 9, 22, 23
Psalm 125

Related:
Isaiah 35.4–7a
Psalm 146

James 2.1–10 [11–13] 14–17
Mark 7.24–end

3rd Service
Psalm 119.57–72
Jonah 3.10—4.11
or Ecclesiasticus 27.30—28.9
Revelation 8.1–5

2nd Service
Psalm 119.41–56 [or 119.49–56]
Exodus 14.5–end
Matthew 6.1–18

Monday

6 September — G
Allen Gardiner, missionary, founder of the South American Mission Society, 1851
DEL week 23

Holy Communion
Colossians 1.24—2.3
Psalm 62.1–7
Luke 6.6–11

Morning Prayer
Psalms 27, **30**
Zechariah 10
Mark 11.1–11

Evening Prayer
Psalms 26, **28**, 29
1 Kings 8.31–62
Acts 16.6–24

Tuesday

7 September — G

Colossians 2.6–15
Psalm 8
Luke 6.12–19

Psalms 32, **36**
Zechariah 11.4–end
Mark 11.12–26

Psalm **33**
1 Kings 8.63—9.9
Acts 16.25–end

Wednesday

8 September — Gw
Birth of the Blessed Virgin Mary
(see p.81)
Accession of King Charles III, 2022
(see p.87)

Colossians 3.1–11
Psalm 15
Luke 6.20–26

Psalm **34**
Zechariah 12.1–10
Mark 11.27–end

Psalm 119.33–56
1 Kings 10.1–25
Acts 17.1–15

Thursday

9 September — G
Charles Fuge Lowder, priest, 1880

Colossians 3.12–17
Psalm 149.1–5
Luke 6.27–38

Psalm **37***
Zechariah 13
Mark 12.1–12

Psalms 39, **40**
1 Kings 11.1–13
Acts 17.16–end

Friday

10 September — G

1 Timothy 1.1–2, 12–14
Psalm 16
Luke 6.39–42

Psalm **31**
Zechariah 14.1–11
Mark 12.13–17

Psalm **35**
1 Kings 11.26–end
Acts 18.1–21

Saturday

11 September — G

1 Timothy 1.15–17
Psalm 113
Luke 6.43–end

Psalms 41, **42**, 43
Zechariah 14.12–end
Mark 12.18–27

Psalms 45, **46**
1 Kings 12.1–24
Acts 18.22—19.7

Trinity 16

Day		Principal Service	3rd Service	2nd Service
Sunday	**12 September** G **16th Sunday after Trinity** Proper 19	*Continuous:* Proverbs 1.20–33 Psalm 19 [or 19.1–6] or *Canticle:* Wisdom 7.26—8.1 *Related:* Isaiah 50.4–9a Psalm 116.1–8 James 3.1–12 Mark 8.27–end	Psalm 119.105–120 Isaiah 44.24—45.8 Revelation 12.1–12	Psalm 119.73–88 [or 119.73–80] Exodus 18.13–26 Matthew 7.1–14
		Holy Communion	**Morning Prayer**	**Evening Prayer**
Monday	**13 September** G John Chrysostom, bishop, teacher of the faith, 407 (see p.82) DEL week 24	1 Timothy 2.1–8 Psalm 28 Luke 7.1–10	Psalm **44** Ecclesiasticus 1.1–10 or Ezekiel 1.1–14 Mark 12.28–34	Psalms **47**, 49 1 Kings 12.25—13.10 Acts 19.8–20 *or:* 1st EP of Holy Cross Day: Psalm 66; Isaiah 52.13—end of 53; Ephesians 2.11–end
		Principal Service	**3rd Service**	**2nd Service**
Tuesday	**14 September** R Holy Cross Day	Numbers 21.4–9 Psalm 22.23–28 Philippians 2.6–11 John 3.13–17	MP Psalms 2, 8, 146 Genesis 3.1–15 John 12.27–36a	EP Psalms 110, 150 Isaiah 63.1–16 1 Corinthians 1.18–25
		Holy Communion	**Morning Prayer**	**Evening Prayer**
Wednesday	**15 September** Gr Cyprian, bishop, martyr, 258 (see p.81)	1 Timothy 3.14–end Psalm 111.1–5 Luke 7.36–end	Psalm **119.57–80** Ecclesiasticus 2 or Ezekiel 2.3—3.11 Mark 13.1–13	Psalms **59**, 60, (67) 1 Kings 17 Acts 20.1–16
Thursday	**16 September** Gw Ninian, bishop, apostle of the Picts, c.432 (see p.84) Edward Bouverie Pusey, priest, 1882	1 Timothy 4.12–end Psalm 111.6–end Luke 7.36–end	Psalms 56, **57**, (63*) Ecclesiasticus 3.17–29 or Ezekiel 3.12–end Mark 13.14–23	Psalms 61, **62**, 64 1 Kings 18.1–20 Acts 20.17–end
Friday	**17 September** Gw Hildegard, abbess, visionary, 1179 (see p.84)	1 Timothy 6.2b–12 Psalm 49.1–9 Luke 8.1–3	Psalms **51**, 54 Ecclesiasticus 4.11–28 or Ezekiel 8 Mark 13.24–31	Psalm **38** 1 Kings 18.21–end Acts 21.1–16
Saturday	**18 September** G	1 Timothy 6.13–16 Psalm 100 Luke 8.4–15	Psalm **68** Ecclesiasticus 4.29—6.1 or Ezekiel 9 Mark 13.32–end	Psalms 65, **66** 1 Kings 19 Acts 21.17–36

Trinity 17

		Principal Service	3rd Service	2nd Service
Sunday	**19 September** G **17th Sunday after Trinity** Proper 20	*Continuous:* Proverbs 31.10–end Psalm 1	Psalm 119.153–end Isaiah 45.9–22 Revelation 14.1–5	Psalm 119.137–152 [or 119.137–144] Exodus 19.10–end Matthew 8.23–end
		Related: Wisdom 1.16—2.1, 12–22 or Jeremiah 11.18–20 Psalm 54 James 3.13—4.3, 7–8a Mark 9.30–37		
		Holy Communion	**Morning Prayer**	**Evening Prayer**
Monday	**20 September** Gr John Coleridge Patteson, bishop, and companions, martyrs, 1871 (see p.81) DEL week 25	Ezra 1.1–6 Psalm 126 Luke 8.16–18	Psalm 71 Ecclesiasticus 6.14–end or Ezekiel 10.1–19 Mark 14.1–11	Psalms 72, 75 1 Kings 21 Acts 21.37—22.21
				or: 1st EP of Matthew, Apostle and Evangelist: Psalm 34; Isaiah 33.13–17; Matthew 6.19–end
		Principal Service	**3rd Service**	**2nd Service**
Tuesday	**21 September** R Matthew, Apostle and Evangelist	Proverbs 3.13–18 Psalm 119.65–72 2 Corinthians 4.1–6 Matthew 9.9–13	MP Psalms 49, 117 1 Kings 19.15–end 2 Timothy 3.14–end	EP Psalm 119.33–40, 89–96 Ecclesiastes 5.4–12 Matthew 19.16–end
		Holy Communion	**Morning Prayer**	**Evening Prayer**
Wednesday	**22 September** G Ember Day	Ezra 9.5–9 *Canticle:* Song of Tobit or Psalm 103.1–6 Luke 9.1–6	Psalm 77 Ecclesiasticus 10.6–8, 12–24 or Ezekiel 12.1–16 Mark 14.26–42	Psalms 119.81–104 1 Kings 22.29–45 Acts 23.12–end
Thursday	**23 September** G	Haggai 1.1–8 Psalm 149.1–5 Luke 9.7–9	Psalm 78.1–39* Ecclesiasticus 11.7–28 or Ezekiel 12.17–end Mark 14.43–52	Psalm 78.40–end* 2 Kings 1.2–17 Acts 24.1–23
Friday	**24 September** G Ember Day	Haggai 1.15b–2.9 Psalm 43 Luke 9.18–22	Psalm 55 Ecclesiasticus 14.20—15.10 or Ezekiel 13.1–16 Mark 14.53–65	Psalm 69 2 Kings 2.1–18 Acts 24.24—25.12
Saturday	**25 September** Gw Lancelot Andrewes, bishop, spiritual writer, 1626 (see p.83) Sergei of Radonezh, monastic reformer, teacher of the faith, 1392 Ember Day	Zechariah 2.1–5, 10–11 Psalm 125 or *Canticle:* Jeremiah 31.10–13 Luke 9.43b–45	Psalms 76, 79 Ecclesiasticus 15.11–end or Ezekiel 14.1–11 Mark 14.66–end	Psalms 81, 84 2 Kings 4.1–37 Acts 25.13–end

Trinity 18

		Principal Service		3rd Service	2nd Service
Sunday	26 September 18th Sunday after Trinity Proper 21　G	*Continuous:* Esther 7.1–6, 9, 10; 9.20–22 Psalm 124	*Related:* Numbers 11.4–6, 10–16, 24–29 Psalm 19.7–end James 5.13–end Mark 9.38–end	Psalm 122 Isaiah 48.12–end Luke 11.37–end	Psalms 120, 121 Exodus 24 Matthew 9.1–8
		Holy Communion		Morning Prayer	Evening Prayer
Monday	27 September Vincent de Paul, founder of the Lazarists, 1660 (see p.84) DEL week 26　Gw	Zechariah 8.1–8 Psalm 102.12–22 Luke 9.46–50		Psalms **80**, 82 Ecclesiasticus 16.17–end or Ezekiel 14.12–end Mark 15.1–15	Psalms **85**, 86 2 Kings 5 Acts 26.1–23
Tuesday	28 September　G	Zechariah 8.20–end Psalm 87 Luke 9.51–56		Psalms 87, **89.1–18** Ecclesiasticus 17.1–24 or Ezekiel 18.1–20 Mark 15.16–32	Psalm **89.19–end** 2 Kings 6.1–23 Acts 26.24–end or: 1st EP of Michael and All Angels: Psalm 91; 2 Kings 6.8–17; Matthew 18.1–6, 10
		Principal Service		3rd Service	2nd Service
Wednesday	29 September Michael and All Angels　W	Genesis 28.10–17 or Revelation 12.7–12 Psalm 103.19–end Revelation 12.7–12 or Hebrews 1.5–end John 1.47–end		MP Psalms 34, 150 Tobit 12.6–end or Daniel 12.1–4 Acts 12.1–11	EP Psalms 138, 148 Daniel 10.4–end Revelation 5
		Holy Communion		Morning Prayer	Evening Prayer
Thursday	30 September　G *Jerome, translator, teacher of the faith, 420*	Nehemiah 8.1–12 Psalm 19.7–11 Luke 10.1–12		Psalms 90, **92** Ecclesiasticus 19.4–17 or Ezekiel 20.1–20 Mark 15.42–end	Psalm **94** 2 Kings 9.17–end Acts 27.27–end
Friday	1 October　G *Remigius, bishop, 533* *Anthony Ashley Cooper (Earl of Shaftesbury), social reformer, 1885*	Baruch 1.15–end or Deuteronomy 31.7–13 Psalm 79.1–9 Luke 10.13–16		Psalms **88**, (95) Ecclesiasticus 19.20–end or Ezekiel 20.21–38 Mark 16.1–8	Psalm **102** 2 Kings 12.1–19 Acts 28.1–16
Saturday	2 October　G	Baruch 4.5–12, 27–29 or Joshua 22.1–6 Psalm 69.33–37 Luke 10.17–24		Psalms 96, **97**, 100 Ecclesiasticus 21.1–17 or Ezekiel 24.15–end Mark 16.9–end	Psalm **104** 2 Kings 17.1–23 Acts 28.17–end

Trinity 19

		Principal Service	3rd Service	2nd Service
Sunday	**3 October** G 19th Sunday after Trinity Proper 22	Continuous: Job 1.1; 2.1–10 Psalm 26 *Related:* Genesis 2.18–24 Psalm 8 Hebrews 1.1–4; 2.5–12 Mark 10.2–16	Psalms 123, 124 Isaiah 49.13–23 Luke 12.1–12	Psalms 125, 126 Joshua 3.7–end Matthew 10.1–22
		Holy Communion	**Morning Prayer**	**Evening Prayer**
Monday	**4 October** Gw Francis of Assisi, friar, deacon, 1226 (see p.84) DEL week 27	Jonah 1.1—2.2, 10 Canticle: Jonah 2.2–4, 7 or Psalm 69.1–6 Luke 10.25–37	Psalms 98, 99, 101 Ecclesiasticus 22.6–22 or Ezekiel 28.1–19 John 13.1–11	Psalm 105* (or 103) 2 Kings 17.24–end Philippians 1.1–11
Tuesday	**5 October** G	Jonah 3 Psalm 130 Luke 10.38–end	Psalm 106* (or 103) Ecclesiasticus 22.27—23.15 or Ezekiel 33.1–20 John 13.12–20	Psalm 107* 2 Kings 18.1–12 Philippians 1.12–end
Wednesday	**6 October** Gr William Tyndale, translator, martyr, 1536 (see p.81)	Jonah 4 Psalm 86.1–9 Luke 11.1–4	Psalms 110, 111, 112 Ecclesiasticus 24.1–22 or Ezekiel 33.21–end John 13.21–30	Psalm 119.129–152 2 Kings 18.13–end Philippians 2.1–13
Thursday	**7 October** G	Malachi 3.13—4.2a Psalm 1 Luke 11.5–13	Psalms 113, 115 Ecclesiasticus 24.23–end or Ezekiel 34.1–16 John 13.31–end	Psalms 114, 116, 117 2 Kings 19.1–19 Philippians 2.14–end
Friday	**8 October** G	Joel 1.13–15, 2.1–2 Psalm 9.1–7 Luke 11.15–26	Psalm 139 Ecclesiasticus 27.30—28.9 or Ezekiel 34.17–end John 14.1–14	Psalms 130, 131, 137 2 Kings 19.20–36 Philippians 3.1—4.1
Saturday	**9 October** G Denys, bishop, and companions, martyrs, c.250 Robert Grosseteste, bishop, philosopher, scientist, 1253	Joel 3.12–end Psalm 97.1, 8–end Luke 11.27–28	Psalms 120, 121, 122 Ecclesiasticus 28.14–end or Ezekiel 36.16–36 John 14.15–end	Psalm 118 2 Kings 20 Philippians 4.2–end

Trinity 20

		Principal Service	3rd Service	2nd Service
Sunday	**10 October** G **20th Sunday after Trinity** Proper 23	*Continuous:* Job 23.1–9, 16–end Psalm 22.1–15 *Related:* Amos 5.6–7, 10–15 Psalm 90.12–end Hebrews 4.12–end Mark 10.17–31	Psalms 129, 130 Isaiah 50.4–10 Luke 13.22–30	Psalms 127 [128] Joshua 5.13—6.20 Matthew 11.20–end
		Holy Communion	**Morning Prayer**	**Evening Prayer**
Monday	**11 October** G Ethelburga, abbess, 675 James the Deacon, companion of Paulinus, 7th cent. DEL week 28	Romans 1.1–7 Psalm 98 Luke 11.29–32	Psalms 123, 124, 125, **126** Ecclesiasticus 31.1–11 or Ezekiel 37.1–14 John 15.1–11	Psalms **127**, 128, 129 2 Kings 21.1–18 1 Timothy 1.1–17
Tuesday	**12 October** Gw Wilfrid, bishop, missionary, 709 (see p.84) Elizabeth Fry, prison reformer, 1845 Edith Cavell, nurse, 1915	Romans 1.16–25 Psalm 19.1–4 Luke 11.37–41	Psalms **132**, 133 Ecclesiasticus 34.9–end or Ezekiel 37.15–end John 15.12–17	Psalms (134), **135** 2 Kings 22.1—23.3 1 Timothy 1.18—end of 2
Wednesday	**13 October** Gw Edward the Confessor, king, 1066 (see p.85)	Romans 2.1–11 Psalm 62.1–8 Luke 11.42–46	Psalm 119.**153–end** Ecclesiasticus 35 or Ezekiel 39.21–end John 15.18–end	Psalm **136** 2 Kings 23.4–25 1 Timothy 3
Thursday	**14 October** G	Romans 3.21–30 Psalm 130 Luke 11.47–end	Psalms 143, 146 Ecclesiasticus 37.7–24 or Ezekiel 43.1–12 John 16.1–15	Psalms **138**, 140, 141 2 Kings 23.36—24.17 1 Timothy 4
Friday	**15 October** Gw Teresa of Avila, teacher of the faith, 1582 (see p.82)	Romans 4.1–8 Psalm 32 Luke 12.1–7	Psalms 142, **144** Ecclesiasticus 38.1–14 or Ezekiel 44.4–16 John 16.16–22	Psalm **145** 2 Kings 24.18—25.12 1 Timothy 5.1–16
Saturday	**16 October** G Nicholas Ridley and Hugh Latimer, bishops, martyrs, 1555	Romans 4.13, 16–18 Psalm 105.6–10, 41–44 Luke 12.8–12	Psalm **147** Ecclesiasticus 38.24–end or Ezekiel 47.1–12 John 16.23–end	Psalms **148**, 149, 150 2 Kings 25.22–end 1 Timothy 5.17–end

Trinity 21

		Principal Service	3rd Service	2nd Service
Sunday 17 October 21st Sunday after Trinity Proper 24	G	*Continuous:* Job 38.1–7 [34–end] Psalm 104.1–10, 26, 37c [or 104.1–10] *Related:* Isaiah 53.4–end Psalm 91.9–end Hebrews 5.1–10 Mark 10.35–45	Psalms 133, 134, 137.1–6 Isaiah 54.1–14 Luke 13.31–end	Psalm 141 Joshua 14.6–14 Matthew 12.1–21 *or:* 1st EP of Luke the Evangelist: Psalm 33; Hosea 6.1–3; 2 Timothy 3.10 – end
Monday 18 October Luke the Evangelist	R	Isaiah 35.3–6 or Acts 16.6–12a Psalm 147.1–7 2 Timothy 4.5–17 Luke 10.1–9	MP Psalms 145, 146 Isaiah 55 Luke 1.1–4	EP Psalm 103 Ecclesiasticus 38.1–14 or Isaiah 61.1–6 Colossians 4.7–end
		Holy Communion	**Morning Prayer**	**Evening Prayer**
Tuesday 19 October Henry Martyn, translator, missionary, 1812 (see p.84) DEL week 29	Gw	Romans 5.12, 15, 17–end Psalm 40.7–12 Luke 12.35–38	Psalms 5, 6 (8) Ecclesiasticus 39.13–end or Ecclesiastes 2 John 17.6–19	Psalms 9, 10* Judith 5.1—6.4 or Exodus 29.38—30.16 1 Timothy 6.11–end
Wednesday 20 October	G	Romans 6.12–18 Psalm 124 Luke 12.39–48	Psalm 119.1–32 Ecclesiasticus 42.15–end or Ecclesiastes 3.1–15 John 17.20–end	Psalms 11, 12, 13 Judith 6.10—7.7 or Leviticus 8 2 Timothy 1.1–14
Thursday 21 October	G	Romans 6.19–end Psalm 1 Luke 12.49–53	Psalms 14, 15, 16 Ecclesiasticus 43.1–12 or Ecclesiastes 3.16—end of 4 John 18.1–11	Psalm 18* Judith 7.19–end or Leviticus 9 2 Timothy 1.15—2.13
Friday 22 October	G	Romans 7.18–end Psalm 119.33–40 Luke 12.54–end	Psalms 17, 19 Ecclesiasticus 43.13–end or Ecclesiastes 5 John 18.12–27	Psalm 22 Judith 8.9–end or Leviticus 16.2–24 2 Timothy 2.14–end
Saturday 23 October	G	Romans 8.1–11 Psalm 24.1–6 Luke 13.1–9	Psalms 20, 21, 23 Ecclesiasticus 44.1–15 or Ecclesiastes 6 John 18.28–end	Psalms 24, 25 Judith 9 or Leviticus 17 2 Timothy 3

Last after Trinity

		Principal Service	3rd Service	2nd Service
Sunday	**24 October** G Last Sunday after Trinity Proper 25	*Continuous:* Job 42.1–6, 10–end Psalm 34.1–8, 19–end [or 34.1–8]	*Related:* Jeremiah 31.7–9 Psalm 126 Hebrews 7.23–end Mark 10.46–end	Psalm 119.89–104 Isaiah 59.9–20 Luke 14.1–14	Psalm 119.121–136 Ecclesiastes 11, 12 2 Timothy 2.1–7 HC Luke 18.9–14
or **Sunday**	**24 October** G Bible Sunday	Isaiah 55.1–11 Psalm 19.7–end 2 Timothy 3.14—4.5 John 5.36b–end		Psalm 119.89–104 Isaiah 45.22–end Matthew 24.30–35 *or* Luke 14.1–14	Psalm 119.1–16 2 Kings 22 Colossians 3.12–17 HC Luke 4.14–30

or, if the date of dedication of a church is not known, the Dedication Festival (Gold or W) may be celebrated today or on 3 October, or on a suitable date chosen locally (see p.80).

		Holy Communion	Morning Prayer	Evening Prayer
Monday	**25 October** G *Crispin and Crispinian, martyrs, c.287* DEL week 30	Romans 8.12–17 Psalm 68.1–6, 19 Luke 13.10–17	Psalms 27, 30 Ecclesiasticus 44.19–45.5 *or* Ecclesiastes 7.1–14 John 19.1–16	Psalms 26, 28, 29 Judith 10 *or* Leviticus 19.1–18, 30–end 2 Timothy 4.1–8
Tuesday	**26 October** Gw *Alfred, king, scholar, 899 (see p.85)* *Cedd, abbot, bishop, 664*	Romans 8.18–25 Psalm 126 Luke 13.18–21	Psalms 32, 36 Ecclesiasticus 45.6–17 *or* Ecclesiastes 7.15–end John 19.17–30	Psalm 33 Judith 11 *or* Leviticus 23.1–22 2 Timothy 4.9–end
Wednesday	**27 October** G	Romans 8.26–30 Psalm 13 Luke 13.22–30	Psalm 34 Ecclesiasticus 46.1–10 *or* Ecclesiastes 8 John 19.31–end	Psalm 119.33–56 Judith 12 *or* Leviticus 23.23–end Titus 1 *or:* 1st EP of Simon and Jude, Apostles: Psalms 124, 125, 126; Deuteronomy 32.1–4; John 14.15–26

		Principal Service	3rd Service	2nd Service
Thursday	**28 October** R Simon and Jude, Apostles	Isaiah 28.14–16 Psalm 119.89–96 Ephesians 2.19–end John 15.17–end	MP Psalms 116, 117 Wisdom 5.1–16 *or* Isaiah 45.18–end Luke 6.12–16	EP Psalm 119.1–16 1 Maccabees 2.42–66 *or* Jeremiah 3.11–18 Jude 1–4, 17–end

		Holy Communion	Morning Prayer	Evening Prayer
Friday	**29 October** Gr *James Hannington, bishop, martyr, 1885 (see p.81)*	Romans 9.1–5 Psalm 147.13–end Luke 14.1–6	Psalm 31 Ecclesiasticus 51.1–12 *or* Ecclesiastes 11.1–8 John 20.1–18	Psalm 35 Judith 15.1–13 *or* Leviticus 25.1–24 Titus 3

4 before Advent / All Saints' Day

All Saints' Day is celebrated on Monday 1 November or on Sunday 31 October; if the latter, there may be a supplementary celebration on 1 November.

If All Saints' Day is celebrated on Monday 1 November only:

			Holy Communion	Morning Prayer	Evening Prayer
Saturday	30 October	G	Romans 11.1–2, 11–12, 25–29 Psalm 94.14–19 Luke 14.1, 7–11	Psalms 41, **42**, 43 Ecclesiasticus 51.13–end or Ecclesiastes 11.9—end of 12 John 20.19–end	Psalms 45, **46** Judith 15.14—end of 16 or Numbers 6.1–5, 21–end Philemon
			Principal Service	**3rd Service**	**2nd Service**
Sunday	31 October 4th Sunday before Advent	R/G	Deuteronomy 6.1–9 Psalm 119.1–8 Hebrews 9.11–14 Mark 12.28–34	Psalms 112, 149 Jeremiah 31.31–34 1 John 3.1–3	1st EP of All Saints' Day Psalms 1, 5 Ecclesiasticus 44.1–15 or Isaiah 40.27–end Revelation 19.6–10
Monday	1 November **All Saints' Day**	Gold or W	Wisdom 3.1–9 or Isaiah 25.6–9 Psalm 24.1–6 Revelation 21.1–6a John 11.32–44	MP Psalms 15, 84, 149 Isaiah 35 Luke 9.18–27	EP Psalms 148, 150 Isaiah 65.17–end Hebrews 11.32—12.2

4 before Advent / All Saints' Day

If All Saints' Day is celebrated on Sunday 31 October only:

			Holy Communion	Morning Prayer	Evening Prayer
Saturday	30 October	G	Romans 11.1–2, 11–12, 25–29 Psalm 94.14–19 Luke 14.1, 7–11	Psalms 41, **42**, 43 Ecclesiasticus 51.13–end or Ecclesiastes 11.9—end of 12 John 20.19–end	**1st EP of All Saints' Day** Psalms 1, 5 Ecclesiasticus 44.1–15 or Isaiah 40.27–end Revelation 19.6–10
			Principal Service	**3rd Service**	**2nd Service**
Sunday	31 October **All Saints' Day**	Gold or W	Wisdom 3.1–9 or Isaiah 25.6–9 Psalm 24.1–6 Revelation 21.1–6a John 11.32–44	MP Psalms 15, 84, 149 Isaiah 35 Luke 9.18–27	EP Psalms 148, 150 Isaiah 65.17–end Hebrews 11.32—12.2
			Holy Communion	**Morning Prayer**	**Evening Prayer**
Monday	1 November DEL week 31	R/G	Romans 11.29–end Psalm 69.31–37 Luke 14.12–14	Psalms **2**, 146 or **44** Isaiah 1.1–20 Matthew 1.18–end	Psalms **92**, 96, 97 or **47**, 49 Daniel 1 Revelation 1

Or, if All Saints' Day is celebrated on Monday 1 November in addition to Sunday 31 October:

			Principal Service	3rd Service	2nd Service
Monday	1 November **All Saints' Day**	Gold or W	Isaiah 56.3–8 or 2 Esdras 2.42–end Psalm 33.1–5 Hebrews 12.18–24 Matthew 5.1–12	MP Psalms 111, 112, 117 Wisdom 5.1–16 or Jeremiah 31.31–34 2 Corinthians 4.5–12	EP Psalm 145 Isaiah 66.20–23 Colossians 1.9–14

4 before Advent

		Holy Communion	Morning Prayer	Evening Prayer
Tuesday	**2 November** Rp/Gp Commemoration of the Faithful Departed (All Souls' Day) DEL week 31	Romans 12.5–16 Psalm 131 Luke 14.15–24 *Lesser Festival eucharistic lectionary:* Lamentations 3.17–26 or Wisdom 3.1–9 Psalm 23 or 27.1–6, 16–end Romans 5.5–11 or 1 Peter 1.3–9 John 5.19–25 or John 6.37–40	Psalms **5**, 147.1–12 or **48**, 52 Isaiah 1.21–end Matthew 2.1–15	Psalms 98, 99, **100** or **50** Daniel 2.1–24 Revelation 2.1–11
Wednesday	**3 November** Rw/Gw Richard Hooker, priest, teacher of the faith, 1600 (see p.82) *Martin of Porres, friar, 1639*	Romans 13.8–10 Psalm 112 Luke 14.25–33	Psalms **9**, 147.13–end or **119.57–80** Isaiah 2.1–11 Matthew 2.16–end	Psalm 111, **112**, 116 or **59**, 60, (67) Daniel 2.25–end Revelation 2.12–end
Thursday	**4 November** R/G	Romans 14.7–12 Psalm 27.14–end Luke 15.1–10	Psalms 11, **15**, 148 or 56, **57**, (63*) Isaiah 2.12–end Matthew 3	Psalm **118** or 61, **62**, 64 Daniel 3.1–18 Revelation 3.1–13
Friday	**5 November** R/G	Romans 15.14–21 Psalm 98 Luke 16.1–8	Psalms **16**, 149 or **51**, 54 Isaiah 3.1–15 Matthew 4.1–11	Psalms 137, 138, **143** or **38** Daniel 3.19–end Revelation 3.14–end
Saturday	**6 November** R/G *Leonard, hermit, 6th cent.* *William Temple, archbishop,* *teacher of the faith, 1944*	Romans 16.3–9, 16, 22–end Psalm 145.1–7 Luke 16.9–15	Psalms **18.31–end**, 150 or **68** Isaiah 4.2—5.7 Matthew 4.12–22	Psalm **145** or 65, **66** Daniel 4.1–18 Revelation 4

3 before Advent

		Principal Service	3rd Service	2nd Service
Sunday	**7 November** R/G **3rd Sunday before Advent**	Jonah 3.1–5, 10 Psalm 62.5–end Hebrews 9.24–end Mark 1.14–20	Psalm 136 Micah 4.1–5 Philippians 4.6–9	Psalms 46 [82] Isaiah 10.33—11.9 John 14.1–29 (or 23–29)
		Holy Communion	**Morning Prayer**	**Evening Prayer**
Monday	**8 November** Rw/Gw Saints and martyrs of England DEL week 32	Wisdom 1.1–7 or Titus 1.1–9 Psalm 139.1–9 or 24.1–6 Luke 17.1–6 *Lesser Festival eucharistic lectionary:* Isaiah 61.4–9 or Ecclesiasticus 44.1–15 Psalm 15 Revelation 19.5–10 John 17.18–23	Psalms 19, **20** or **71** Isaiah 5.8–24 Matthew 4.23—5.12	Psalm **34** or **72**, 75 Daniel 4.19–end Revelation 5
Tuesday	**9 November** R/G *Margery Kempe, mystic, c.1440*	Wisdom 2.23—3.9 or Titus 2.1–8, 11–14 Psalm 34.1–6 or 37.3–5, 30–32 Luke 17.7–10	Psalms **21**, 24 or **73** Isaiah 5.25–end Matthew 5.13–20	Psalms 36, **40** or **74** Daniel 5.1–12 Revelation 6
Wednesday	**10 November** Rw/Gw Leo the Great, bishop, teacher of the faith, 461 (see p.82)	Wisdom 6.1–11 or Titus 3.1–7 Psalm 82 or 23 Luke 17.11–19	Psalms **23**, 25 or **77** Isaiah 6 Matthew 5.21–37	Psalm **37** or **119.81–104** Daniel 5.13–end Revelation 7.1–4, 9–end
Thursday	**11 November** Rw/Gw Martin, bishop, c.397 (see p.83)	Wisdom 7.22—8.1 or Philemon 7–20 Psalm 119.89–96 or 146.4–end Luke 17.20–25	Psalms **26**, 27 or **78.1–39* Isaiah 7.1–17 Matthew 5.38–end	Psalms 42, **43** or **78.40–end*** Daniel 6 Revelation 8
Friday	**12 November** R/G	Wisdom 13.1–9 or 2 John 4–9 Psalm 19.1–4 or 119.1–8 Luke 17.26–end	Psalms 28, **32** or **55** Isaiah 8.1–15 Matthew 6.1–18	Psalm **31** or **69** Daniel 7.1–14 Revelation 9.1–12
Saturday	**13 November** Rw/Gw Charles Simeon, priest, evangelical divine, 1836 (see p.83)	Wisdom 18.14–16, 19.6–9 or 3 John 5–8 Psalm 105.1–5, 35–42 or 112 Luke 18.1–8	Psalm **33** or **76**, 79 Isaiah 8.16—9.7 Matthew 6.19–end	Psalms 84, **86** or 81, **84** Daniel 7.15–end Revelation 9.13–end

2 before Advent

		Principal Service	3rd Service	2nd Service
Sunday	**14 November** R/G **2nd Sunday before Advent** *Remembrance Sunday*	Daniel 12.1–3 Psalm 16 Hebrews 10.11–14 [15–18] 19–25 Mark 13.1–8	Psalm 96 1 Samuel 9.27—10.2a; 10.17–26 Matthew 13.31–35	Psalm 95 Daniel 3 [or 3.13–end] Matthew 13.24–30, 36–43
		Holy Communion	**Morning Prayer**	**Evening Prayer**
Monday	**15 November** R/G DEL week 33	1 Maccabees 1.10–15, 41–43, 54–57, 62–64 or Revelation 1.1–4, 2.1–5 Psalm 79.1–5 or 1 Luke 18.35–end	Psalms 46, 47 or 80, 82 Isaiah 9.8—10.4 Matthew 7.1–12	Psalms 70, 71 or 85, 86 Daniel 8.1–14 Revelation 10
Tuesday	**16 November** Rw/Gw Margaret, queen, philanthropist, 1093 (see p.85) *Edmund Rich, archbishop, 1240*	2 Maccabees 6.18–end or Revelation 3.1–6, 14–31 Psalm 11 or 15 Luke 19.1–10	Psalms 48, 52 or 87, 89.1–18 Isaiah 10.5–19 Matthew 7.13–end	Psalms 67, 72 or 89.19–end Daniel 8.15–end Revelation 11.1–14
Wednesday	**17 November** Rw/Gw Hugh, bishop, 1200 (see p.83)	2 Maccabees 7.1, 20–31 or Revelation 4 Psalm 116.10–end or 150 Luke 19.11–28	Psalms 56, 57 or 119.105–128 Isaiah 10.20–32 Matthew 8.1–13	Psalm 73 or 91, 93 Daniel 9.1–19 Revelation 11.15–end
Thursday	**18 November** Rw/Gw Elizabeth, princess, philanthropist, 1231 (see p.85)	1 Maccabees 2.15–29 or Revelation 5.1–10 Psalm 129 or 149.1–5 Luke 19.41–44	Psalms 61, 62 or 90, 92 Isaiah 10.33—11.9 Matthew 8.14–22	Psalms 74, 76 or 94 Daniel 9.20–end Revelation 12
Friday	**19 November** Rw/Gw Hilda, abbess, 680 (see p.84) *Mechtild, béguine, mystic, 1280*	1 Maccabees 4.36–37, 52–59 or Revelation 10.8–11 Psalm 122 or 119.65–72 Luke 19.45–48	Psalms 63, 65 or 88, (95) Isaiah 11.10—end of 12 Matthew 8.23–end	Psalm 77 or 102 Daniel 10.1—11.1 Revelation 13.1–10
Saturday	**20 November** R/Gr Edmund, king, martyr, 870 (see p.81) *Priscilla Lydia Sellon, a restorer of the religious life in the Church of England, 1876*	1 Maccabees 6.1–13 or Revelation 11.4–12 Psalm 124 or 144.1–9 Luke 20.27–40	Psalm 78.1–39 or 96, 97, 100 Isaiah 13.1–13 Matthew 9.1–17	Psalm 78.40–end or 104 Daniel 12 Revelation 13.11–end or: 1st EP of Christ the King: Psalms 99, 100; Isaiah 10.33—11.9; 1 Timothy 6.11–16

Christ the King / Sunday next before Advent

			Principal Service	3rd Service	2nd Service
Sunday	**21 November** **Christ the King** Sunday next before Advent	R/W	Daniel 7.9–10, 13, 14 Psalm 93 Revelation 1.4b–8 John 18.33–37	MP Psalms 29, 110 Isaiah 32.1–8 Revelation 3.7–end	EP Psalm 72 [or 72.1–7] Daniel 5 John 6.1–15
			Holy Communion	**Morning Prayer**	**Evening Prayer**
Monday	**22 November** *Cecilia, martyr, c.230* DEL week 34	R/G	Daniel 1.1–6, 8–20 *Canticle:* Bless the Lord Luke 21.1–4	Psalms 92, **96** or **98**, 99, 101 Isaiah 14.3–20 Matthew 9.18–34	Psalms **80**, 81 or **105*** (or 103) Isaiah 40.1–11 Revelation 14.1–13
Tuesday	**23 November** *Clement, bishop, martyr, c.100 (see p.81)*	R/Gr	Daniel 2.31–45 *Canticle:* Benedicite 1–3 Luke 21.5–11	Psalms **97**, 98, 100 or **106*** (or 103) Isaiah 17 Matthew 9.35—10.15	Psalms 99, **101** or **107*** Isaiah 40.12–26 Revelation 14.14—end of 15
Wednesday	**24 November**	R/G	Daniel 5.1–6, 13–14, 16–17, 23–28 *Canticle:* Benedicite 4–5 Luke 21.12–19	Psalms 110, 111, **112** or 110, **111**, 112 Isaiah 19 Matthew 10.16–33	Psalms 121, **122**, 123, 124 or **119.129–152** Isaiah 40.27—41.7 Revelation 16.1–11
Thursday	**25 November** *Catherine, martyr, 4th cent.* *Isaac Watts, hymn writer, 1748*	R/G	Daniel 6.12–end *Canticle:* Benedicite 6–8a Luke 21.20–28	Psalms **125**, 126, 127, 128 or 113, **115** Isaiah 21.1–12 Matthew 10.34—11.1	Psalms 131, 132, **133** or 114, **116,** 117 Isaiah 41.8–20 Revelation 16.12–end
Friday	**26 November**	R/G	Daniel 7.2–14 *Canticle:* Benedicite 8b–10a Luke 21.29–33	Psalm **139** or **139** Isaiah 22.1–14 Matthew 11.2–19	Psalms **146**, 147 or **130**, 131, 137 Isaiah 41.21—42.9 Revelation 17
Saturday	**27 November**	R/G	Daniel 7.15–27 *Canticle:* Benedicite 10b–end Luke 21.34–36	Psalm **145** or 120, **121**, 122 Isaiah 24 Matthew 11.20–end	Psalms 148, **149**, **150** or **118** Isaiah 42.10–17 Revelation 18

¶ Additional Weekday Lectionary

This Additional Weekday Lectionary provides two readings for each day of the year, except for Sundays, Principal Feasts and other Principal Holy Days, Holy Week and Festivals (for which the readings provided in the main body of this lectionary are used). The readings for 'first evensongs' in the main body of the lectionary are used on the eves of Principal Feasts and may be used on the eves of Festivals. This lectionary is intended particularly for use in those places of worship that attract occasional rather than daily worshippers, and can be used either at Morning or Evening Prayer. Psalmody is not provided and should be taken from the daily provision earlier in this volume.

29 November – Advent 1

Monday	30 November	Andrew the Apostle – see p.10	
Tuesday	1 December	Zephaniah 3.14–end	1 Thessalonians 4.13–end
Wednesday	2 December	Isaiah 65.17—66.2	Matthew 24.1–14
Thursday	3 December	Micah 5.2–5a	John 3.16–21
Friday	4 December	Isaiah 66.18–end	Luke 13.22–30
Saturday	5 December	Micah 7.8–15	Romans 15.30—16.7, 25–end

6 December – Advent 2

Monday	7 December	Jeremiah 7.1–11	Philippians 4.4–9
Tuesday	8 December	Daniel 7.9–14	Matthew 24.15–28
Wednesday	9 December	Amos 9.11–end	Romans 13.8–end
Thursday	10 December	Jeremiah 23.5–8	Mark 11.1–11
Friday	11 December	Jeremiah 33.14–22	Luke 21.25–36
Saturday	12 December	Zechariah 14.4–11	Revelation 22.1–7

13 December – Advent 3

Monday	14 December	Isaiah 40.1–11	Matthew 3.1–12
Tuesday	15 December	Lamentations 3.22–33	1 Corinthians 1.1–9
Wednesday	16 December	Joel 3.9–16	Matthew 24.29–35
Thursday	17 December	Ecclesiasticus 24.1–9	1 Corinthians 2.1–13
		or Proverbs 8.22–31	
Friday	18 December	Exodus 3.1–6	Acts 7.20–36
Saturday	19 December	Isaiah 11.1–9	Romans 15.7–13

20 December – Advent 4

Monday	21 December	Numbers 24.15b–19	Revelation 22.10–21
Tuesday	22 December	Jeremiah 30.7–11a	Acts 4.1–12
Wednesday	23 December	Isaiah 7.10–15	Matthew 1.18–23
Thursday	24 December	At Evening Prayer the readings for Christmas Eve are used.	
		At other services, the following readings are used:	
		Isaiah 29.13–18	1 John 4.7–16
Friday	25 December	**Christmas Day** see p.13	
Saturday	26 December	Stephen, deacon, first martyr – see p.13	

27 December – John, Apostle and Evangelist

Monday	28 December	The Holy Innocents – see p.14	
Tuesday	29 December	Micah 1.1–4; 2.12–13	Luke 2.1–7
Wednesday	30 December	Isaiah 9.2–7	John 8.12–20
Thursday	31 December	Ecclesiastes 3.1–13	Revelation 21.1–8
		or 1st EP of Naming and Circumcision of Jesus	
Friday	1 January	Naming and Circumcision of Jesus – see p.15	
Saturday	2 January	Isaiah 66.6–14	Matthew 12.46–50
		If, for pastoral reasons, **The Epiphany** is celebrated on Sunday	
		3 January, the readings for the Eve of Epiphany are used at Evening Prayer.	

3 January – Christmas 2 / The Epiphany

Monday	**4 January**	Isaiah 63.7–16	Galatians 3.23—4.7
		or, if, for pastoral reasons, **The Epiphany** *is celebrated on Sunday 3 January, the following readings are used:*	
		Deuteronomy 6.4–15	John 10.31–end
Tuesday	**5 January**	*At Evening Prayer the readings for the Eve of the Epiphany are used. At other services, the following readings are used:*	
		Isaiah 12	2 Corinthians 2.12–end
		or, if, for pastoral reasons, **The Epiphany** *is celebrated on Sunday 3 January, the following readings are used:*	
		Isaiah 63.7–16	Galatians 3.23—4.7
Wednesday	**6 January**	**The Epiphany** – see p.16	
		or, if, for pastoral reasons, **The Epiphany** *is celebrated on Sunday 3 January, the following readings are used:*	
		Isaiah 12	2 Corinthians 2.12–end
Thursday	**7 January**	Genesis 25.19–end	Ephesians 1.1–6
Friday	**8 January**	Joel 2.28–end	Ephesians 1.7–14
Saturday	**9 January**	*At Evening Prayer the readings for the Eve of the Baptism of Christ are used.*	
		At other services, the following readings are used:	
		Proverbs 8.12–21	Ephesians 1.15–end

10 January – Baptism of Christ (Epiphany 1)

Monday	**11 January**	Isaiah 41.14–20	John 1.29–34
Tuesday	**12 January**	Exodus 17.1–7	Acts 8.26–end
Wednesday	**13 January**	Exodus 15.1–19	Colossians 2.8–15
Thursday	**14 January**	Zechariah 6.9–15	1 Peter 2.4–10
Friday	**15 January**	Isaiah 51.7–16	Galatians 6.14–18
Saturday	**16 January**	Leviticus 16.11–22	Hebrews 10.19–25

17 January – Epiphany 2

Monday	**18 January**	1 Kings 17.8–16	Mark 8.1–10
Tuesday	**19 January**	1 Kings 19.1–9a	Mark 1.9–15
Wednesday	**20 January**	1 Kings 19.9b–18	Mark 9.2–13
Thursday	**21 January**	Leviticus 11.1–8, 13–19, 41–45	Acts 10.9–16
Friday	**22 January**	Isaiah 49.8–13	Acts 10.34–43
Saturday	**23 January**	Genesis 35.1–15	Acts 10.44–end

24 January – Epiphany 3

Monday	**25 January**	Conversion of Paul – see p.20	
Tuesday	**26 January**	Ezekiel 20.39–44	John 17.20–end
Wednesday	**27 January**	Nehemiah 2.1–10	Romans 12.1–8
Thursday	**28 January**	Deuteronomy 26.16–end	Romans 14.1–9
Friday	**29 January**	Leviticus 19.9–28	Romans 15.1–7
Saturday	**30 January**	*If, for pastoral reasons, the* **Presentation of Christ** *is celebrated on Sunday 31 January the readings for the Eve of the Presentation are used. At other services, the following readings are used:*	
		Jeremiah 33.1–11	1 Peter 5.5b–end

31 January – Epiphany 4 / Presentation

Monday	**1 February**	Jonah 3	2 Corinthians 5.11–21
		If the **Presentation of Christ** *is celebrated on Tuesday 2 February, the readings for the Eve of the Presentation are used at Evening Prayer.*	
Tuesday	**2 February**	**Presentation of Christ** – see p.21	
		or, if, for pastoral reasons, the **Presentation of Christ** *is celebrated on Sunday 31 January, the following readings are used:*	
		Proverbs 4.10–end	Matthew 5.13–20
Wednesday	**3 February**	Isaiah 61.1–9	Luke 7.18–30
Thursday	**4 February**	Isaiah 52.1–12	Matthew 10.1–15
Friday	**5 February**	Isaiah 56.1–8	Matthew 28.16–end
Saturday	**6 February**	Habakkuk 2.1–4	Revelation 14.1–7

		7 February – Next before Lent	
Monday	8 February	2 Kings 2.13–22	3 John
Tuesday	9 February	Judges 14.5–17	Revelation 10.4–11
Wednesday	10 February	**Ash Wednesday** – see p.23	
Thursday	11 February	Genesis 2.7–end	Hebrews 2.5–end
Friday	12 February	Genesis 4.1–12	Hebrews 4.12–end
Saturday	13 February	2 Kings 22.11–end	Hebrews 5.1–10
		14 February – Lent 1	
Monday	15 February	Genesis 6.11–end, 7.11–16	Luke 4.14–21
Tuesday	16 February	Deuteronomy 31.7–13	1 John 3.1–10
Wednesday	17 February	Genesis 11.1–9	Matthew 24.15–28
Thursday	18 February	Genesis 13.1–13	1 Peter 2.13–end
Friday	19 February	Genesis 21.1–8	Luke 9.18–27
Saturday	20 February	Genesis 32.22–32	2 Peter 1.10–end
		21 February – Lent 2	
Monday	22 February	1 Chronicles 21.1–17	1 John 2.1–8
Tuesday	23 February	Zechariah 3	2 Peter 2.1–10a
Wednesday	24 February	Job 1.1–22	Luke 21.34—22.6
Thursday	25 February	2 Chronicles 29.1–11	Mark 11.15–19
Friday	26 February	Exodus 19.1–9a	1 Peter 1.1–9
Saturday	27 February	Exodus 19.9b–19	Acts 7.44–50
		28 February – Lent 3	
Monday	1 March	Joshua 4.1–13	Luke 9.1–11
Tuesday	2 March	Exodus 15.22–27	Hebrews 10.32–end
Wednesday	3 March	Genesis 9.8–17	1 Peter 3.18–end
Thursday	4 March	Daniel 12.5–end	Mark 13.21–end
Friday	5 March	Numbers 20.1–13	1 Corinthians 10.23–end
Saturday	6 March	Isaiah 43.14–end	Hebrews 3.1–15
		7 March – Lent 4	
Monday	8 March	2 Kings 24.18—25.7	1 Corinthians 15.20–34
Tuesday	9 March	Jeremiah 13.12–19	Acts 13.26–35
Wednesday	10 March	Jeremiah 13.20–27	1 Peter 1.17—2.3
Thursday	11 March	Jeremiah 22.11–19	Luke 11.37–52
Friday	12 March	Jeremiah 17.1–14	Luke 6.17–26
Saturday	13 March	Ezra 1	2 Corinthians 1.12–19
		14 March – Lent 5	
Monday	15 March	Joel 2.12–17	2 John
Tuesday	16 March	Isaiah 58.1–14	Mark 10.32–45
Wednesday	17 March	Job 36.1–12	John 14.1–14
Thursday	18 March	Jeremiah 9.17–22 *or* 1st EP of Joseph of Nazareth	Luke 13.31–35
Friday	19 March	Joseph of Nazareth – see p.28	
Saturday	20 March	Job 17.6–end	John 12.27–36
		From the Monday of Holy Week until Easter Eve the seasonal lectionary is used: see pp.29–30.	
		28 March – Easter	
Monday	29 March	Isaiah 54.1–14	Romans 1.1–7
Tuesday	30 March	Isaiah 51.1–11	John 5.19–29
Wednesday	31 March	Isaiah 26.1–19	John 20.1–10
Thursday	1 April	Isaiah 43.14–21	Revelation 1.4–end
Friday	2 April	Isaiah 42.10–17	1 Thessalonians 5.1–11
Saturday	3 April	Job 14.1–14	John 21.1–14
		4 April – Easter 2	
Monday	5 April	**Annunciation of Our Lord to the Blessed Virgin Mary** – see p.32	
Tuesday	6 April	Proverbs 8.1–11	Acts 16.6–15
Wednesday	7 April	Hosea 5.15—6.6	1 Corinthians 15.1–11
Thursday	8 April	Jonah 2	Mark 4.35–end
Friday	9 April	Genesis 6.9–end	1 Peter 3.8–end
Saturday	10 April	1 Samuel 2.1–8	Matthew 28.8–15

11 April – Easter 3

Monday	12 April	Exodus 24.1–11	Revelation 5
Tuesday	13 April	Leviticus 19.9–18, 32–end	Matthew 5.38–end
Wednesday	14 April	Genesis 3.8–21	1 Corinthians 15.12–28
Thursday	15 April	Isaiah 33.13–22	Mark 6.47–end
Friday	16 April	Nehemiah 9.6–17	Romans 5.12–end
Saturday	17 April	Isaiah 61.10—62.5	Luke 24.1–12

18 April – Easter 4

Monday	19 April	Jeremiah 31.10–17	Revelation 7.9–end
Tuesday	20 April	Job 31.13–23	Matthew 7.1–12
Wednesday	21 April	Genesis 2.4b–9	1 Corinthians 15.35–49
Thursday	22 April	Proverbs 28.3–end	Mark 10.17–31
		or 1st EP of George	
Friday	23 April	George, Martyr, patron of England – see p.34	
Saturday	24 April	1 Chronicles 29.10–13	Luke 24.13–35

25 April – Easter 5

Monday	26 April	Mark the Evangelist – see p.35 (transferred from 25 April)	
Tuesday	27 April	Deuteronomy 8.1–10	Matthew 6.19–end
Wednesday	28 April	Hosea 13.4–14	1 Corinthians 15.50–end
Thursday	29 April	Exodus 3.1–15	Mark 12.18–27
Friday	30 April	Ezekiel 36.33–end	Romans 8.1–11
		or 1st EP of Philip and James	
Saturday	1 May	Philip and James, Apostles – see p.35	

2 May – Easter 6

Monday	3 May	Proverbs 4.1–13	Philippians 2.1–11
Tuesday	4 May	Isaiah 32.12–end	Romans 5.1–11
Wednesday	5 May	At Evening Prayer, the readings for the Eve of Ascension Day are used.	
		At other services, the following readings are used:	
		Isaiah 43.1–13	Titus 2.11—3.8
Thursday	6 May	**Ascension Day** – see p.36	
Friday	7 May	Exodus 35.30—36.1	Galatians 5.13–end
Saturday	8 May	Numbers 11.16–17, 24–29	1 Corinthians 2

9 May – Easter 7

Monday	10 May	Numbers 27.15–end	1 Corinthians 3
Tuesday	11 May	1 Samuel 10.1–10	1 Corinthians 12.1–13
Wednesday	12 May	1 Kings 19.1–18	Matthew 3.13–end
Thursday	13 May	Ezekiel 11.14–20	Matthew 9.35—10.20
		or 1st EP of Matthias	
Friday	14 May	Matthias the Apostle – see p.37	
Saturday	15 May	At Evening Prayer, the readings for the Eve of Pentecost are used.	
		At other services, the following readings are used:	
		Micah 3.1–8	Ephesians 6.10–20

16 May – Pentecost

Monday	17 May	Genesis 12.1–9	Romans 4.13–end
Tuesday	18 May	Genesis 13.1–12	Romans 12.9–end
Wednesday	19 May	Genesis 15	Romans 4.1–8
Thursday	20 May	Genesis 22.1–18	Hebrews 11.8–19
Friday	21 May	Isaiah 51.1–8	John 8.48–end
Saturday	22 May	At Evening Prayer the readings for the Eve of Trinity Sunday are used.	
		At other services, the following readings are used:	
		Ecclesiasticus 44.19–23	James 2.14–26
		or Joshua 2.1–15	

23 May – Trinity Sunday

Monday	24 May	Exodus 2.1–10	Hebrews 11.23–31
Tuesday	25 May	Exodus 2.11–end	Acts 7.17–29
Wednesday	26 May	Exodus 3.1–12	Acts 7.30–38
		or 1st EP of Corpus Christi	
Thursday	27 May	Day of Thanksgiving for the Institution of the Holy Communion	
		(Corpus Christi) – see p.40	
		or, where Corpus Christi is not celebrated as a Festival:	
		Exodus 6.1–13	John 9.24–38
Friday	28 May	Exodus 34.1–10	Mark 7.1–13
Saturday	29 May	Exodus 34.27–end	2 Corinthians 3.7–end

Additional Weekday Lectionary

		30 May – Trinity 1	
Monday	31 May	The Visit of the Blessed Virgin Mary to Elizabeth – see p.41	
Tuesday	1 June	Genesis 41.15–40	Mark 13.1–13
Wednesday	2 June	Genesis 42.17–end	Matthew 18.1–14
Thursday	3 June	Genesis 45.1–15	Acts 7.9–16
Friday	4 June	Genesis 47.1–12	1 Thessalonians 5.12–end
Saturday	5 June	Genesis 50.4–21	Luke 15.11–end
		6 June – Trinity 2	
Monday	7 June	Isaiah 32	James 3.13–end
Tuesday	8 June	Proverbs 3.1–18	Matthew 5.1–12
Wednesday	9 June	Judges 6.1–16	Matthew 5.13–24
Thursday	10 June	Jeremiah 6.9–15 *or* 1st EP of Barnabas	1 Timothy 2.1–6
Friday	11 June	Barnabas the Apostle – see p.42	
Saturday	12 June	Isaiah 6.1–9	Revelation 19.9–end
		13 June – Trinity 3	
Monday	14 June	Exodus 13.13b–end	Luke 15.1–10
Tuesday	15 June	Proverbs 1.20–end	James 5.13–end
Wednesday	16 June	Isaiah 5.8–24	James 1.17–25
Thursday	17 June	Isaiah 57.14–end	John 13.1–17
Friday	18 June	Jeremiah 15.15–end	Luke 16.19–31
Saturday	19 June	Isaiah 25.1–9	Acts 2.22–33
		20 June – Trinity 4	
Monday	21 June	Exodus 20.1–17	Matthew 6.1–15
Tuesday	22 June	Proverbs 6.6–19	Luke 4.1–14
Wednesday	23 June	Isaiah 24.1–15 *or* 1st EP of Birth of John the Baptist	1 Corinthians 6.1–11
Thursday	24 June	Birth of John the Baptist – see p.44	
Friday	25 June	Jeremiah 20.7–end	Matthew 27.27–44
Saturday	26 June	Job 28	Hebrews 11.32—12.2
		27 June – Trinity 5	
Monday	28 June	Exodus 32.1–14 *or* 1st EP of Peter and Paul, Apostles (*or* Peter the Apostle)	Colossians 3.1–11
Tuesday	29 June	Peter and Paul, Apostles *or* Peter the Apostle – see p.45	
Wednesday	30 June	Isaiah 26.1–9	Romans 8.12–27
Thursday	1 July	Jeremiah 8.18—9.6	John 13.21–35
Friday	2 July	2 Samuel 5.1–12 *or* 1st EP of Thomas the Apostle	Matthew 27.45–56
Saturday	3 July	Thomas the Apostle – see p.46	
		4 July – Trinity 6	
Monday	5 July	Exodus 40.1–16	Luke 14.15–24
Tuesday	6 July	Proverbs 11.1–12	Mark 12.38–44
Wednesday	7 July	Isaiah 33.2–10	Philippians 1.1–11
Thursday	8 July	Job 38	Luke 18.1–14
Friday	9 July	Job 42.1–6	John 3.1–15
Saturday	10 July	Ecclesiastes 9.1–11	Hebrews 1.1–9
		11 July – Trinity 7	
Monday	12 July	Numbers 23.1–12	1 Corinthians 1.10–17
Tuesday	13 July	Proverbs 12.1–12	Galatians 3.1–14
Wednesday	14 July	Isaiah 49.8–13	2 Corinthians 8.1–11
Thursday	15 July	Hosea 14	John 15.1–17
Friday	16 July	2 Samuel 18.18–end	Matthew 27.57–66
Saturday	17 July	Isaiah 55.1–7	Mark 16.1–8

	18 July – Trinity 8		
Monday	19 July	Joel 3.16–21	Mark 4.21–34
Tuesday	20 July	Proverbs 12.13–end	John 1.43–51
Wednesday	21 July	Isaiah 55.8–end	2 Timothy 2.8–19
		or 1st EP of Mary Magdalene	
Thursday	22 July	Mary Magdalene – see p.49	
Friday	23 July	Jeremiah 14.1–9	Luke 8.4–15
Saturday	24 July	Ecclesiastes 5.10–19	1 Timothy 6.6–16
		or 1st EP of James the Apostle	
	25 July – James / Trinity 9		
Monday	26 July	Joshua 1.1–9	1 Corinthians 9.19–end
		or James the Apostle transferred – see p.50	
Tuesday	27 July	Proverbs 15.1–11	Galatians 2.15–end
Wednesday	28 July	Isaiah 49.1–7	1 John 1
Thursday	29 July	Proverbs 27.1–12	John 15.12–27
Friday	30 July	Isaiah 59.8–end	Mark 15.6–20
Saturday	31 July	Zechariah 7.8—8.8	Luke 20.27–40
	1 August – Trinity 10		
Monday	2 August	Judges 13.1–23	Luke 10.38–42
Tuesday	3 August	Proverbs 15.15–end	Matthew 15.21–28
Wednesday	4 August	Isaiah 45.1–7	Ephesians 4.1–16
Thursday	5 August	Jeremiah 16.1–15	Luke 12.35–48
		or 1st EP of The Transfiguration	
Friday	6 August	The Transfiguration of Our Lord – see p.52	
Saturday	7 August	Jeremiah 26.1–19	Ephesians 3.1–13
	8 August – Trinity 11		
Monday	9 August	Ruth 2.1–13	Luke 10.25–37
Tuesday	10 August	Proverbs 16.1–11	Philippians 3.4b–end
Wednesday	11 August	Deuteronomy 11.1–21	2 Corinthians 9.6–end
Thursday	12 August	Ecclesiasticus 2	
		or Ecclesiastes 2.12–25	John 16.1–15
Friday	13 August	Obadiah 1–10	John 19.1–16
Saturday	14 August	2 Kings 2.11–14	Luke 24.36–end
		or 1st EP of The Blessed Virgin Mary	
	15 August – The Blessed Virgin Mary / Trinity 12		
Monday	16 August	1 Samuel 17.32–50	Matthew 8.14–22
		or The Blessed Virgin Mary transferred – see p.54	
Tuesday	17 August	Proverbs 17.1–15	Luke 7.1–17
Wednesday	18 August	Jeremiah 5.20–end	2 Peter 3.8–end
Thursday	19 August	Daniel 2.1–23	Luke 10.1–20
Friday	20 August	Daniel 3.1–28	Revelation 15
Saturday	21 August	Daniel 6	Philippians 2.14–24
	22 August – Trinity 13		
Monday	23 August	2 Samuel 7.4–17	2 Corinthians 5.1–10
		or 1st EP of Bartholomew the Apostle	
Tuesday	24 August	Bartholomew the Apostle – see p.56	
Wednesday	25 August	Judges 4.1–10	Romans 1.8–17
Thursday	26 August	Isaiah 49.14–end	John 16.16–24
Friday	27 August	Job 9.1–24	Mark 15.21–32
Saturday	28 August	Exodus 19.1–9	John 20.11–18
	29 August – Trinity 14		
Monday	30 August	Haggai 1	Mark 7.9–23
Tuesday	31 August	Proverbs 21.1–18	Mark 6.30–44
Wednesday	1 September	Hosea 11.1–11	1 John 4.9–end
Thursday	2 September	Lamentations 3.34–48	Romans 7.14–end
Friday	3 September	1 Kings 19.4–18	1 Thessalonians 3
Saturday	4 September	Ecclesiasticus 4.11–28	
		or Deuteronomy 29.2–15	2 Timothy 3.10–end

5 September – Trinity 15

Monday	6 September	Wisdom 6.12–21 or Job 12.1–16	Matthew 15.1–9
Tuesday	7 September	Proverbs 8.1–11	Luke 6.39–end
Wednesday	8 September	Proverbs 2.1–15	Colossians 1.9–20
Thursday	9 September	Baruch 3.14–end or Genesis 1.1–13	John 1.1–18
Friday	10 September	Ecclesiasticus 1.1–20 or Deuteronomy 7.7–16	1 Corinthians 1.18–end
Saturday	11 September	Wisdom 9.1–12 or Jeremiah 1.4–10	Luke 2.41–end

12 September – Trinity 16

Monday	13 September	Genesis 21.1–13 or 1st EP of Holy Cross Day	Luke 1.26–38
Tuesday	14 September	Holy Cross Day – see p.59	
Wednesday	15 September	2 Kings 4.1–7	John 2.1–11
Thursday	16 September	2 Kings 4.25b–37	Mark 3.19b–35
Friday	17 September	Judith 8.9–17, 28–36 or Ruth 1.1–18	John 19.25b–30
Saturday	18 September	Exodus 15.19–27	Acts 1.6–14

19 September – Trinity 17

Monday	20 September	Exodus 19.16–end or 1st EP of Matthew, Apostle and Evangelist	Hebrews 12.18–end
Tuesday	21 September	Matthew, Apostle and Evangelist – see p.60	
Wednesday	22 September	1 Chronicles 29.10–19	Colossians 3.12–17
Thursday	23 September	Nehemiah 8.1–12	1 Corinthians 14.1–12
Friday	24 September	Isaiah 1.10–17	Mark 12.28–34
Saturday	25 September	Daniel 6.6–23	Revelation 12.7–12

26 September – Trinity 18

Monday	27 September	2 Samuel 22.4–7, 17–20	Hebrews 7.26—8.6
Tuesday	28 September	Proverbs 22.17–end or 1st EP of Michael and All Angels	2 Corinthians 12.1–10
Wednesday	29 September	Michael and All Angels – see p.61	
Thursday	30 September	Isaiah 24.1–15	John 16.25–33
Friday	1 October	Jeremiah 14.1–9	Luke 23.44–56
Saturday	2 October	Zechariah 8.14–end	John 20.19–end

3 October – Trinity 19

Monday	4 October	1 Kings 3.3–14	1 Timothy 3.14—4.8
Tuesday	5 October	Proverbs 27.11–end	Galatians 6.1–10
Wednesday	6 October	Isaiah 51.1–6	2 Corinthians 1.1–11
Thursday	7 October	Ecclesiasticus 18.1–14 or Job 26	1 Corinthians 11.17–end
Friday	8 October	Ecclesiasticus 28.2–12 or Job 19.21–end	Mark 15.33–47
Saturday	9 October	Isaiah 44.21–end	John 21.15–end

10 October – Trinity 20

Monday	11 October	1 Kings 6.2–10	John 12.1–11
Tuesday	12 October	Proverbs 31.10–end	Luke 10.38–42
Wednesday	13 October	Jonah 1	Luke 5.1–11
Thursday	14 October	Exodus 12.1–20	1 Thessalonians 4.1–12
Friday	15 October	Isaiah 64	Matthew 27.45–56
Saturday	16 October	2 Samuel 7.18–end	Acts 2.22–33

17 October – Trinity 21

Monday	18 October	Luke the Evangelist – see p.64	
Tuesday	19 October	Ecclesiastes 11	Luke 13.10–17
Wednesday	20 October	Hosea 14.1–7	2 Timothy 4.1–8
Thursday	21 October	Isaiah 49.1–7	John 19.16–25a
Friday	22 October	Proverbs 24.3–22	John 8.1–11
Saturday	23 October	Ecclesiasticus 7.8–17, 32–end or Deuteronomy 6.16–25	2 Timothy 1.1–14

24 October – Last after Trinity

Monday	**25 October**	Isaiah 42.14–21	Luke 1.5–25
Tuesday	**26 October**	1 Samuel 4.12–end	Luke 1.57–end
Wednesday	**27 October**	Baruch 5 *or* Haggai 1.1–11	Mark 1.1–11
		or 1st EP of Simon and Jude, Apostles	
Thursday	**28 October**	Simon and Jude, Apostles – see p.65	
Friday	**29 October**	2 Samuel 11.1–17	Matthew 14.1–12
Saturday	**30 October**	Isaiah 43.15–21	Acts 19.1–10
		or 1st EP of **All Saints' Day**, *if All Saints' Day is celebrated on 31 October*	

31 October – 4 before Advent / All Saints' Day

Monday	**1 November**	**All Saints' Day** – see pp.66–67	
		Or, if All Saints' Day is celebrated on 31 October only, the following readings are used:	
		Esther 3.1–11, 4.7–17	Matthew 18.1–10
Tuesday	**2 November**	Ezekiel 18.21–end	Matthew 18.12–20
Wednesday	**3 November**	Proverbs 3.27–end	Matthew 18.21–end
Thursday	**4 November**	Exodus 23.1–9	Matthew 19.1–15
Friday	**5 November**	Proverbs 3.13–18	Matthew 19.16–end
Saturday	**6 November**	Deuteronomy 28.1–6	Matthew 20.1–16

7 November – 3 before Advent

Monday	**8 November**	Isaiah 40.21–end	Romans 11.25–end
Tuesday	**9 November**	Ezekiel 34.20–end	John 10.1–18
Wednesday	**10 November**	Leviticus 26.3–13	Titus 2.1–10
Thursday	**11 November**	Hosea 6.1–6	Matthew 9.9–13
Friday	**12 November**	Malachi 4	John 4.5–26
Saturday	**13 November**	Micah 6.6–8	Colossians 3.12–17

14 November – 2 before Advent (Remembrance Sunday)

Monday	**15 November**	Micah 7.1–7	Matthew 10.24–39
Tuesday	**16 November**	Habakkuk 3.1–19*a*	1 Corinthians 4.9–16
Wednesday	**17 November**	Zechariah 8.1–13	Mark 13.3–8
Thursday	**18 November**	Zechariah 10.6–end	1 Peter 5.1–11
Friday	**19 November**	Micah 4.1–5	Luke 9.28–36
Saturday	**20 November**	At Evening Prayer the readings for the Eve of Christ the King are used.	
		At other services, the following readings are used:	
		Exodus 16.1–21	John 6.3–15

21 November – Christ the King (Sunday next before Advent)

Monday	**22 November**	Jeremiah 30.1–3, 10–17	Romans 12.9–21
Tuesday	**23 November**	Jeremiah 30.18–24	John 10.22–30
Wednesday	**24 November**	Jeremiah 31.1–9	Matthew 15.21–31
Thursday	**25 November**	Jeremiah 31.10–17	Matthew 16.13–end
Friday	**26 November**	Jeremiah 31.31–37	Hebrews 10.11–18
Saturday	**27 November**	Isaiah 51.17—52.2	Ephesians 5.1–20

¶ Collects and Post Communions

All the contemporary language Collects and Post Communions, including the Additional Collects, may be found in *Common Worship: Collects and Post Communions* (Church House Publishing: London, 2004). The Additional Collects are also published separately.

The contemporary language Collects and Post Communions all appear in *Times and Seasons: President's Edition for Holy Communion*. Apart from the Additional Collects, they appear in the other Common Worship volumes as follows:

- ¶ President's edition: all Collects and Post Communions;
- ¶ *Daily Prayer*: all Collects;
- ¶ main volume: Collects, Additional Collects and Post Communions for Sundays, Principal Feasts and Holy Days, and Festivals;
- ¶ *Festivals*: Collects and Post Communions for Festivals, Lesser Festivals, Common of the Saints and Special Occasions.

The traditional-language Collects and Post Communions all appear in the president's edition. They appear in other publications as follows:

- ¶ main volume: Collects and Post Communions for Sundays, Principal Feasts and Holy Days, and Festivals;
- ¶ separate booklet: Collects and Post Communions for Lesser Festivals, Common of the Saints and Special Occasions.

¶ Lectionary for Dedication Festival

If date not known, observe on the first Sunday in October or Last Sunday after Trinity.

Evening Prayer on the Eve
Psalm 24
2 Chronicles 7.11–16
John 4.19–29

Dedication Festival
Gold or White

	Principal Service	**3rd Service**	**2nd Service**	**Psalmody**
Year A	1 Kings 8.22–30 *or* Revelation 21.9–14 Psalm 122 Hebrews 12.18–24 Matthew 21.12–16	Haggai 2.6–9 Hebrews 10.19–25	Jeremiah 7.1–11 1 Corinthians 3.9–17 *HC* Luke 19.1–10	MP 48, 150 EP 132
Year B	Genesis 28.11–18 *or* Revelation 21.9–14 Psalm 122 1 Peter 2.1–10 John 10.22–29	Haggai 2.6–9 Hebrews 10.19–25	Jeremiah 7.1–11 Luke 19.1–10	MP 48, 150 EP 132
Year C	1 Chronicles 29.6–19 Psalm 122 Ephesians 2.19–end John 2.13–22	Haggai 2.6–9 Hebrews 10.19–25	Jeremiah 7.1–11 Luke 19.1–10	MP 48, 150 EP 132

Lectionary for Common of the Saints

The Blessed Virgin Mary

Genesis 3.8–15, 20; Isaiah 7.10–14; Micah 5.1–4
Psalms 45.10–17; 113; 131
Acts 1.12–14; Romans 8.18–30; Galatians 4.4–7
Luke 1.26–38; *or* 1.39–47; John 19.25–27

Martyrs

2 Chronicles 24.17–21; Isaiah 43.1–7; Jeremiah 11.18–20; Wisdom 4.10–15
Psalms 3; 11; 31.1–5; 44.18–24; 126
Romans 8.35–end; 2 Corinthians 4.7–15; 2 Timothy 2.3–7 [8–13]; Hebrews 11.32–end;
 1 Peter 4.12–end; Revelation 12.10–12a
Matthew 10.16–22; *or* 10.28–39; *or* 16.24–26; John 12.24–26; *or* 15.18–21

Agnes (21 Jan): *also* Revelation 7.13–end
Alban (22 June): *especially* 2 Timothy 2.3–13; John 12.24–26
Alphege (19 Apr): *also* Hebrews 5.1–4
Boniface (5 June): *also* Acts 20.24–28
Charles (30 Jan): *also* Ecclesiasticus 2.12–end; 1 Timothy 6.12–16
Clement (23 Nov): *also* Philippians 3.17—4.3; Matthew 16.13–19
Cyprian (15 Sept): *especially* 1 Peter 4.12–end; *also* Matthew 18.18–22
Edmund (20 Nov): *also* Proverbs 20.28; 21.1–4, 7
Ignatius (17 Oct): *also* Philippians 3.7–12; John 6.52–58
James Hannington (29 Oct): *especially* Matthew 10.28–39
Janani Luwum (17 Feb): *also* Ecclesiasticus 4.20–28; John 12.24–32
John Coleridge Patteson (20 Sept): *especially* 2 Chronicles 24.17–21; *also* Acts 7.55–end
Justin (1 June): *especially* John 15.18–21; *also* 1 Maccabees 2.15–22; 1 Corinthians 1.18–25
Laurence (10 Aug): *also* 2 Corinthians 9.6–10
Lucy (13 Dec): *also* Wisdom 3.1–7; 2 Corinthians 4.6–15
Oswald (5 Aug): *especially* 1 Peter 4.12–end; John 16.29–end
Perpetua, Felicity and comps (7 Mar): *especially* Revelation 12.10–12a; *also* Wisdom 3.1–7
Polycarp (23 Feb): *also* Revelation 2.8–11
Thomas Becket (29 Dec *or* 7 Jul): *especially* Matthew 10.28–33; *also* Ecclesiasticus 51.1–8
William Tyndale (6 Oct): *also* Proverbs 8.4–11; 2 Timothy 3.12–end

Teachers of the Faith and Spiritual Writers

1 Kings 3.[6–10] 11–14; Proverbs 4.1–9; Wisdom 7.7–10, 15–16; Ecclesiasticus 39.1–10
Psalms 19.7–10; 34.11–17; 37.31–35; 119.89–96; 119.97–104
1 Corinthians 1.18–25; *or* 2.1–10; *or* 2.9–end; Ephesians 3.8–12; 2 Timothy 4.1–8; Titus 2.1–8
Matthew 5.13–19; *or* 13.52–end; *or* 23.8–12; Mark 4.1–9; John 16.12–15

Ambrose (7 Dec): *also* Isaiah 41.9b–13; Luke 22.24–30
Anselm (21 Apr): *also* Wisdom 9.13–end; Romans 5.8–11
Athanasius (2 May): *also* Ecclesiasticus 4.20–28; *also* Matthew 10.24–27
Augustine of Hippo (28 Aug): *especially* Ecclesiasticus 39.1–10; *also* Romans 13.11–13
Basil and Gregory (2 Jan): *especially* 2 Timothy 4.1–8; Matthew 5.13–19
Bernard (20 Aug): *especially* Revelation 19.5–9
Catherine of Siena (29 Apr): *also* Proverbs 8.1, 6–11; John 17.12–end
Francis de Sales (24 Jan): *also* Proverbs 3.13–18; John 3.17–21
Gregory the Great (3 Sept): *also* 1 Thessalonians 2.3–8
Gregory of Nyssa and Macrina (19 July): *especially* 1 Corinthians 2.9–13; *also* Wisdom 9.13–17
Hilary (13 Jan): *also* 1 John 2.18–25; John 8.25–32
Irenaeus (28 June): *also* 2 Peter 1.16–end
Jeremy Taylor (13 Aug); *also* Titus 2.7–8, 11–14
John Bunyan (30 Aug): *also* Hebrews 12.1–2; Luke 21.21, 34–36
John Chrysostom (13 Sept): *especially* Matthew 5.13–19; *also* Jeremiah 1.4–10
John of the Cross (14 Dec): *especially* 1 Corinthians 2.1–10; *also* John 14.18–23
Leo (10 Nov): *also* 1 Peter 5.1–11
Richard Hooker (3 Nov): *especially* John 16.12–15; *also* Ecclesiasticus 44.10–15
Teresa of Avila (15 Oct): *also* Romans 8.22–27
Thomas Aquinas (28 Jan): *especially* Wisdom 7.7–10, 15–16; 1 Corinthians 2.9–end; John 16.12–15
William Law (10 Apr): *especially* 1 Corinthians 2.9–end; *also* Matthew 17.1–9

Bishops and Other Pastors

1 Samuel 16.1, 6–13; Isaiah 6.1–8; Jeremiah 1.4–10; Ezekiel 3.16–21; Malachi 2.5–7
Psalms 1; 15; 16.5–end; 96; 110
Acts 20.28–35; 1 Corinthians 4.1–5; 2 Corinthians 4.1–10 [*or* 1–2, 5–7];
　　or 5.14–20; 1 Peter 5.1–4
Matthew 11.25–end; *or* 24.42–46; John 10.11–16; *or* 15.9–17; *or* 21.15–17

Augustine of Canterbury (26 May): *also* 1 Thessalonians 2.2b–8; Matthew 13.31–33
Charles Simeon (13 Nov): *especially* Malachi 2.5–7; *also* Colossians 1.3–8; Luke 8.4–8
David (1 Mar): *also* 2 Samuel 23.1–4; Psalm 89.19–22, 24
Dunstan (19 May): *especially* Matthew 24.42–46; *also* Exodus 31.1–5
Edward King (8 Mar): *also* Hebrews 13.1–8
George Herbert (27 Feb): *especially* Malachi 2.5–7; Matthew 11.25–end;
　　also Revelation 19.5–9
Hugh (17 Nov); *also* 1 Timothy 6.11–16
John Keble (14 July): *also* Lamentations 3.19–26; Matthew 5.1–8
John and Charles Wesley (24 May): *also* Ephesians 5.15–20
Lancelot Andrewes (25 Sept): *especially* Isaiah 6.1–8
Martin of Tours (11 Nov): *also* 1 Thessalonians 5.1–11; Matthew 25.34–40
Nicholas (6 Dec): *also* Isaiah 61.1–3; 1 Timothy 6.6–11; Mark 10.13–16
Richard (16 June): *also* John 21.15–19
Swithun (15 July): *also* James 5.7–11, 13–18
Thomas Ken (8 June): *especially* 2 Corinthians 4.1–10 [*or* 1–2, 5–7]; Matthew 24.42–46
Wulfstan (19 Jan): *especially* Matthew 24.42–46

Members of Religious Communities

1 Kings 19.9–18; Proverbs 10.27–end; Song of Solomon 8.6–7; Isaiah 61.10—62.5;
Hosea 2.14–15, 19–20
Psalms 34.1–8; 112.1–9; 119.57–64; 123; 131
Acts 4.32–35; 2 Corinthians 10.17—11.2; Philippians 3.7–14; 1 John 2.15–17;
Revelation 19.1, 5–9
Matthew 11.25–end; *or* 19.3–12; *or* 19.23–end; Luke 9.57–end; *or* 12.32–37

Aelred (12 Jan): *also* Ecclesiasticus 15.1–6
Alcuin (20 May): *also* Colossians 3.12–16; John 4.19–24
Antony (17 Jan): *especially* Philippians 3.7–14, *also* Matthew 19.16–26
Bede (25 May): *also* Ecclesiasticus 39.1–10
Benedict (11 July): *also* 1 Corinthians 3.10–11; Luke 18.18–22
Clare (11 Aug): *especially* Song of Solomon 8.6–7
Dominic (8 Aug): *also* Ecclesiasticus 39.1–10
Etheldreda (23 June): *also* Matthew 25.1–13
Francis of Assisi (4 Oct): *also* Galatians 6.14–end; Luke 12.22–34
Hilda (19 Nov): *especially* Isaiah 61.10–62.5
Hildegard (17 Sept): *also* 1 Corinthians 2.9–13; Luke 10.21–24
Julian of Norwich (8 May): *also* 1 Corinthians 13.8–end; Matthew 5.13–16
Vincent de Paul (27 Sept): *also* 1 Corinthians 1.25–end; Matthew 25.34–40

Missionaries

Isaiah 52.7–10; *or* 61.1–3*a*; Ezekiel 34.11–16; Jonah 3.1–5
Psalms 67; *or* 87; *or* 97; *or* 100; *or* 117
Acts 2.14, 22–36; *or* 13.46–49; *or* 16.6–10; *or* 26.19–23; Romans 15.17–21;
2 Corinthians 5.11—6.2
Matthew 9.35–end; *or* 28.16–end; Mark 16.15–20; Luke 5.1–11; *or* 10.1–9

Aidan (31 Aug): *also* 1 Corinthians 9.16–19
Anskar (3 Feb): *especially* Isaiah 52.7–10; *also* Romans 10.11–15
Chad (2 Mar *or* 26 Oct): *also* 1 Timothy 6.11*b*–16
Columba (9 June): *also* Titus 2.11–end
Cuthbert (20 Mar *or* 4 Sept): *especially* Ezekiel 34.11–16; *also* Matthew 18.12–14
Cyril and Methodius (14 Feb): *especially* Isaiah 52.7–10; *also* Romans 10.11–15
Henry Martyn (19 Oct): *especially* Mark 16.15–end; *also* Isaiah 55.6–11
Ninian (16 Sept): *especially* Acts 13.46–49; Mark 16.15–end
Patrick (17 Mar): *also* Psalm 91.1–4, 13–end; Luke 10.1–12, 17–20
Paulinus (10 Oct); *especially* Matthew 28.16–end
Wilfrid (12 Oct): *especially* Luke 5.1–11; *also* 1 Corinthians 1.18–25
Willibrord (7 Nov): *especially* Isaiah 52.7–10; Matthew 28.16–end

Any Saint

General

Genesis 12.1–4; Proverbs 8.1–11; Micah 6.6–8; Ecclesiasticus 2.7–13 [14–end]
Psalms 32; 33.1–5; 119.1–8; 139.1–4 [5–12]; 145.8–14
Ephesians 3.14–19; *or* 6.11–18; Hebrews 13.7–8, 15–16; James 2.14–17;
    1 John 4.7–16; Revelation 21.[1–4] 5–7
Matthew 19.16–21; *or* 25.1–13; *or* 25.14–30; John 15.1–8; *or* 17.20–end

Christian rulers

1 Samuel 16.1–13*a*; 1 Kings 3.3–14
Psalms 72.1–7; 99
1 Timothy 2.1–6
Mark 10.42–45; Luke 14.27–33

Alfred the Great (26 Oct): *also* 2 Samuel 23.1–5; John 18.33–37
Edward the Confessor (13 Oct): *also* 2 Samuel 23.1–5; 1 John 4.13–16
Margaret of Scotland (16 Nov): *also* Proverbs 31.10–12, 20, 26–end;
    1 Corinthians 12.13—13.3; Matthew 25.34–end

Those working for the poor and underprivileged

Isaiah 58.6–11
Psalms 82; 146.5–10
Hebrews 13.1–3; 1 John 3.14–18
Matthew 5.1–12; *or* 25.31–end

Elizabeth of Hungary (18 Nov): *especially* Matthew 25.31–end; *also* Proverbs 31.10–end
Josephine Butler (30 May): *especially* Isaiah 58.6–11; *also* 1 John 3.18–23; Matthew 9.10–13
William Wilberforce, Olaudah Equiano and Thomas Clarkson (30 July): *also* Job 31.16–23;
    Galatians 3.26–end, 4.6–7; Luke 4.16–21

Men and women of learning

Proverbs 8.22–31; Ecclesiasticus 44.1–15
Psalms 36.5–10; 49.1–4
Philippians 4.7–8
Matthew 13.44–46, 52; John 7.14–18

Those whose holiness was revealed in marriage and family life

Proverbs 31.10–13, 19–20, 30–end; Tobit 8.4–7
Psalms 127; 128
1 Peter 3.1–9
Mark 3.31–end; Luke 10.38–end

Mary Sumner (9 Aug): *also* Hebrews 13.1–5
Monica (27 Aug): *also* Ecclesiasticus 26.1–3, 13–16

¶ *Lectionary for Special Occasions*

The Guidance of the Holy Spirit

Proverbs 24.3–7; Isaiah 30.15–21; Wisdom 9.13–17
Psalms 25.1–9; 104.26–33; 143.8–10
Acts 15.23–29; Romans 8:22–27; 1 Corinthians 12.4–13
Luke 14.27–33; John 14.23–26; *or* 16.13–15

Rogation Days
(3–5 May in 2027)

Deuteronomy 8.1–10; 1 Kings 8.35–40; Job 28.1–11
Psalms 104.21–30; 107.1–9; 121
Philippians 4.4–7; 2 Thessalonians 3.6–13; 1 John 5.12–15
Matthew 6.1–15; Mark 11.22–24; Luke 11.5–13

Harvest Thanksgiving

Year A
Deuteronomy 8.7–18 *or* 28.1–14
Psalm 65
2 Corinthians 9.6–end
Luke 12.16–30; *or* 17.11–19

Year B
Joel 2.21–27
Psalm 126
1 Timothy 2.1–7; *or* 6.6–10
Matthew 6.25–33

Year C
Deuteronomy 26.1–11
Psalm 100
Philippians 4.4–9
or Revelation 14.14–18
John 6.25–35

Mission and Evangelism

Isaiah 49.1–6; *or* 52.7–10; Micah 4.1–5
Psalms 2; 46; 67
Acts 17.10–end; 2 Corinthians 5.14—6.2; Ephesians 2.13–end
Matthew 5.13–16; *or* 28.16–end; John 17.20–end

The Unity of the Church

Jeremiah 33.6–9a; Ezekiel 36.23–28; Zephaniah 3.16–end
Psalms 100; 122; 133
Ephesians 4.1–6; Colossians 3.9–17; 1 John 4.9–15
Matthew 18.19–22; John 11.45–52; *or* 17.11b–23

The Peace of the World

Isaiah 9.1–6; *or* 57.15–19; Micah 4.1–5
Psalms 40.14–17; 72.1–7; 85.8–13
Philippians 4.6–9; 1 Timothy 2.1–6; James 3.13–18
Matthew 5.43–end; John 14.23–29; *or* 15.9–17

Social Justice and Responsibility

Isaiah 32.15–end; Amos 5.21–24; *or* 8.4–7; Acts 5.1–11
Psalms 31.21–24; 85.1–7; 146.5–10
Colossians 3.12–15; James 2.1–4
Matthew 5.1–12; *or* 25.31–end; Luke 16.19–end

Ministry, including Ember Days
(See page 7)

Numbers 11.16–17, 24–29; *or* 27.15–end; 1 Samuel 16.1–13*a*; Isaiah 6.1–8;
    or 61.1–3; Jeremiah 1.4–10
Psalms 40.8–13; 84.8–12; 89.19–25; 101.1–5, 7; 122
Acts 20.28–35; 1 Corinthians 3.3–11; Ephesians 4.4–16; Philippians 3.7–14
Luke 4.16–21; *or* 12.35–43; *or* 22.24–27; John 4.31–38; *or* 15.5–17

In Time of Trouble

Genesis 9.8–17; Job 1.13–end; Isaiah 38.6–11
Psalms 86.1–7; 107.4–15; 142.1–7
Romans 3.21–26; Romans 8.18–25; 2 Corinthians 8.1–5, 9
Mark 4.35–end; Luke 12.1–7; John 16.31–end

For the Sovereign

Joshua 1.1–9; Proverbs 8.1–16
Psalms 20; 101; 121
Romans 13.1–10; Revelation 21.22—22.4
Matthew 22.16–22; Luke 22.24–30

The anniversary of HM The King's accession is 8 September.

¶ Psalms in the Course of a Month

The following provision may be used for a monthly cycle of psalmody in place of the psalms provided in the tables in this booklet. It is based on the provision in The Book of Common Prayer.

	Morning Prayer	**Evening Prayer**
1	1—5	6—8
2	9—11	12—14
3	15—17	18
4	19—21	22—23
5	24—26	27—29
6	30—31	32—34
7	35—36	37
8	38—40	41—43
9	44—46	47—49
10	50—52	53—55
11	56—58	59—61
12	62—64	65—67
13	68	69—70
14	71—72	73—74
15	75—77	78
16	79—81	82—85
17	86—88	89
18	90—92	93—94
19	95—97	98—101
20	102—103	104
21	105	106
22	107	108—109
23	110—112	113—115
24	116—118	119.1–32
25	119.33—72	119.73–96
26	119.97—144	119.145—176
27	120—125	126—131
28	132—135	136—138
29	139—140	141—143
30	144—146	147—150

In February the psalms are read only to the 28th or 29th day of the month.

In January, March, May, July, August, October and December, all of which have 31 days, the same psalms are read on the last day of the month (being an ordinary weekday) which were read the day before, or else the psalms of the monthly course omitted on one of the Sundays in that month.